MANUAL FOR
ACCEPTED MISSIONARY CANDIDATES

MANUAL FOR

ACCEPTED MISSIONARY CANDIDATES

Marjorie A. Collins

William Carey Library

533 HERMOSA STREET • SOUTH PASADENA, CALIF. 91030 • TEL. 213-682-2047

Library of Congress Catalog Card Number 72-92749
International Standard Book Number 0-87808-118-6

Published by the William Carey Library
533 Hermosa Street
South Pasadena, California 91030
Telephone 213-682-2047

PRINTED IN THE UNITED STATES OF AMERICA

Lovingly and gratefully dedicated to my
dear friend and faithful intercessor,
ELEANOR LASIER ROWE, R.N.
whose life is a constant challenge to me
to forget those things which are behind
and to reach forth unto those things
which are before.

Contents

Foreword

"WELCOME, RECRUIT!" So, - you're an accepted candidate! You've come a long way, Jim or Jill, - and
you've got a long way yet to go! No doubt, much of it
will be unexplored and unfamiliar territory; how else
could it be? After all, you've just begun to put your
feet "in the Jordan" after quite a thrilling journey
to its banks, and now Canaan remains ahead to be entered. What a challenging prospect!

This book will serve you well as a working guide
and you'll find that its contents are the very essence
of many vital things you will need to know and want to
do in moving ahead from your very special category as
an "accepted candidate". Keeping in mind the valuable
suggestions and ideas laid out for you here could be of
great assistance in the immediate future, with happier,
more profitable plans and preparations for getting to
the field with a little less hectic rush and more pleasant accomplishments.

There may have been some incidents and episodes in
your life up until now that were exciting and demanding,
but you'll find none of them quite the equal of your
present status now that your mission board has given
you the "green light". *Exciting* as can be because so
many new horizons will be opening up to you. *Demanding*
because so many persistent factors in different frame-
works will be cropping up. And all the events and
every circumstance, under the Lord's blessed control,
shaping up together in the perfect pattern He has for
you, and leading on to your own "D" day when you launch
out for Language School or the field.

There's something unusual about being an "accepted candidate". It's a sort of "postlude" to years of family circle, schooling and training, hearing and answering God's call and then application to "the" mission toward which He pointed you. It's a kind of "prelude" to what you expect confidently will be wonderful years of missionary service, in His will.

Now you stand in a peculiar type of "doldrums", betwixt and between things that were and things that will be. It calls for a different kind of understanding of yourself and your continuing walk with the Master of the Harvest. You will need to draw deeply upon His promised resources of physical, psychological and spiritual strength. As you become more and more "detached" in your thinking from connections in the homeland, and contemplate joining up with a new and unknown mission family, there may come a strange feeling of uncertainty, of not really quite "belonging" to anyone or any group in this interval. Healthy individuals usually come through this momentary "sound barrier" quickly and happily as they busy themselves with the things that need doing - right now.

If you now belong to a denominational mission, chances are the matter of finances for your support, equipment, travel, Language School and other items will be taken care of by your Board. That leaves you rather free to visit family and friends, appear at churches of your denomination in a schedule already laid out for you, and make preparations for a fixed departure date, etc. If, on the other hand, you are now part of a so-called "faith" mission, chances are that you will be required to search out all the finances needed to "get going" to the field. At least, this is the traditional manner of operating and procedure for accepted candidates of such undenominational missions.

No doubt, the former arrangement might be considered "ideal" for supporting and sending accepted candidates and has many advantages for working as a missionary with an assured support provided by a denominational treasury. Many thousands of splendid, denominational missionaries have gone to the field under these favorable circumstances. If you enjoy such a prospect, consider yourself fortunate in this "launching stage". I cannot help but feel, however, that there is something very meaningful to be said for the "fried-it-yourself" arrangement of the undenominational mission with its accepted candidates. Some of these mission boards have said, "We can analyze, evaluate and accept the candidate on the merits of his application, recommendations and our interviews. That is our *mission's* approval. Now, as the candidate prays and goes out to find his needed funds for support and other items, that is (to us) *God's* acceptance and seal, through His churches and people, of the candidate."

While the anticipated experience of seeking prayer and financial backing may appear quite harrowing at first glance, once entered into, it becomes a refreshing, constant assurance of God's guidance, care and pre-planned provision. Don't be surprised if some of your most "close-in" contacts fail in producing prayer and fund support. It is natural to think that family and life-long friends will help, and surely your church will sieze the opportunity to back up one of its own young people. Often these closest contacts do respond with joy and enthusiasm, appreciative of your dedication to God's highest purposes for your life and willing to assist practically and faithfully.

On the other hand, sometimes even a father or mother or other close relatives are "turned off" by their own child's going to the mission field, and refuse any aid. Churches who have nurtured children through their Sunday School years and adolescence sometimes sense no privilege or responsibility for supporting this same person as an "accepted candidate". Don't let this "throw you" or change your decision to follow Him at all cost! His promise of Philippians 4:19 will never be more meaningful to you than at such a crisis of disappointment in your hoped-for allegiance by those who know you best.

This period of looking for support, - (of being put up on the "auction block", as one candidate put it) need not be embarrassing or humiliating to you if you "commit your way to the Lord and trust in Him" to bring it to pass." From the most unexpected sources God will give you new friends and helpers to "stand by the stuff" while you go down to battle. Maybe for the first time in your Christian experience, in your helplessness and wonder-

ment, you will find an abundant provision supernaturally
made for you through some previously unknown churches
and friends who will "catch on" to the Spirit's prompt-
ings in their hearts that you are for *them*.   This is one
of the most exhilarating experiences of your young life,
to wait and watch for the next "surprise" that the Lord
will work out for your support, another lovely "handful
of purpose".

So, dear "accepted candidate", encourage your heart,
knowing that you have done the right and noble thing in
obeying His call to the whitened fields.   Believe with
all your mind that "when He putteth forth His sheep He
goeth before" and He is cognizant of every detail concerned with your going out – in *His* good time and *His*
wonderful way.   Accept your new role as an incipient ambassador for Jesus Christ with dignity and spiritual
poise, but without any feeling that you are some special
"breed of cat".

Give your testimony of God's working in your life
with honesty, clarity and brevity.   Don't be afraid to
let out your enthusiasm, and a genuine tear on your cheek
from heartfelt emotion is nothing to be ashamed of.
Strangely you will find that God will move on the hearts
and minds of some in your circle or audience and challenge
them to participate in sending you forth.   It will be His
way of involving them in His great program, allowing their
sharing for your needs to be great blessing.

May I caution you against using high pressure methods
or unseemly manners of presentation in trying to gain
favor with church missionary committees or individuals?
Your dress, your conduct on and off the platform, your
conversation with new acquaintances, your attitudes toward
life and life investment, above all, will influence those
you meet more than you can imagine.   Don't try to be
"over-pious" to impress officials and older adults.   Do
be yourself naturally and sincerely and, as you pray and
"walk worthy of the vocation wherewith you are called",
the Lord will do the rest, mysteriously but satisfyingly.

So now, "accepted candidate", may I commend you to
the Lord and His grace in this new and glorious road of
adventuring with God that you have entered upon.   On your
part, "keep on keeping on" and you will arrive at the

destination He has planned for you. There are greater
things ahead for you than you've ever dreamed - but
they are all part of a fierce battle for the souls of
men.   Remember, you are a soldier, so expect to get
"shot at" by the enemy in many peculiar forms; but, as
"a good soldier of Jesus Christ, endure hardness" because you are in a winning battle with the Captain of
your salvation!

Welcome, recruit! *GLAD YOU ENLISTED!*

CLARENCE W. JONES, LL.D.
Co-Founder and Honorary Chairman of the Board
The World Radio Missionary Fellowship, Inc. (HCJB)

Preface

You are now an accepted missionary candidate. It has been a long road from the day you accepted Jesus Christ as your Savior, then dedicated yourself to His will and purposes for your life. There have been uphill climbs, plateaus of impatience, and times when the downward trail looked very pleasant. But God overruled in all the circumstances which you faced. You chose Him and His way. And now you are about to step out on the greatest adventure of your life, filled with joy, responsibility and the anticipation of unknown tomorrows. You have proven God faithful. You know of a certainty that He is directing you to the Mission Field of His own choosing. And you stand expectantly, waiting for that great day when you will, at last, be on your way to the people among whom you will witness.

Although this volume is written primarily for those who have been accepted by a "Faith Mission" board, may it also provide help to those of you who will serve under denominational leadership.

The purpose of this book is to acquaint you with many of the details that will need to be cared for during this time of walking in "no-man's land" as an accepted missionary candidate. It will cause you to stop and ask questions concerning yourself and your ministry. It will tell you some of the pitfalls you must avoid. It will guide you concerning matters which you must care for during these next weeks and months before departure for the field.

May God grant you, each one, quietness of heart and mind as you await His perfect timing, and may He give you many precious years of fellowship and service in the field of His choice.

1

The Changing
Missionary Image

What is the image reflected in the minds of those who hear the word "missionary"? Is it a vision of a plain-faced lady wearing a funereal expression, speaking strictly of "down-country" activities in the heart of Africa, so concerned about the needs of her little tribe of 300 people that she has forgotten the world around her? Is she speaking in a church which really has little concern for her and her people? Does she drone on endlessly without presenting needs and challenges? Or does she tell a few sad stories, especially about orphans and the awful state of womanhood, receives a good offering, and the meeting is termed a "success"?

There will, of course, always be a place for the full-time missionary evangelist, winning souls to Christ, planting churches, building up the saved in their faith, training national leadership and "gossiping the Gospel" to anyone and everyone with whom he comes into contact. In this day of specialization, however, it is as common to use the title secretary, teacher, engineer, doctor, nurse, musician, printer, script writer, Christian Education worker, administrator, lab technician, language specialist, pilot, announcer, technician, accountant, photographer or journalist as it is to lump them all together and call them missionaries. They are Christian workers going about to do the Lord's work. Their first and foremost responsibility is to live the Gospel of Jesus Christ as they serve in their specialized capacity.

In order to do this, missionaries and candidates have discovered that their person must be as attractive to those to whom they minister as the Gospel itself. The day of the "dowdy" missonary is becoming a thing of the past. We are beginning to realize that missionaries are human beings - men and women - and that they are no different than the dedicated Christian who longs to serve the Lord and give forth the Gospel at home. Most men and women, although avoiding the extreme fashions of the day, wear clothing which is in good taste and carefully selected. A little color in the face has made a difference in the look of the female. Men have taken on a sportier look, have done away with the "funeral black" or "chocolate brown" suit which has always seemed a "must" for the church speaker, and have chosen red, green, blue or orange ties. Women, if they wear hats at all, usually don a small veil since some churches feel this is an essential part of a woman speaker's wardrobe.

The candidate no longer feels it imperative merely to lecture endlessly of his future experiences. He has learned that visual aids of many kinds are acceptable in almost every church, and a presentation with pictures and displays makes a far greater impression upon the listeners. He will be more frank with the congregation. He will allow that there are problems to be met and overcome. He may even confess that he is human and has had to face some difficulties, himself, and will, undoubtedly, face even more on the field.

Today's candidate will seem younger and more worldly-wise than those of other years. He may represent a specialized field of service which is difficult to describe. He will be well prepared in more than one specialty. He may be going to a country very few have heard mentioned especially as new nations emerge in this day of independence. He may have an electronic display with him. He might use a beautifully prepared stereo presentation. His literature will be attractive and well designed.

The candidate will look no different than anyone else in the group. He will be a man of purpose, with goals to be reached and definite tasks to be done. He will be less structured in his thinking and more democratic in his decisions. He will rebel somewhat at strict authority, but will add good ideas to any group. He will

demand the right to fail, and when given responsibility
he will expect to receive some authority. He will have
more psychological preparation than any generation before him. He will not be afraid of change. He will
have greater resources at his disposal. He will be a
conceptual thinker. We are, undoubtedly, entering upon
an era in which we will find the most dedicated, least
self-conscious individuals who will not require the
luxuries of material possessions, but will work for the
cause of Christ in the hardest of circumstances for the
sole purpose of spreading love and peace throughout the
earth. He will be allowed to contribute far more to
the work than others who preceded him. He will be less
visionary, more honest and practical in his Christian
experience and what he will expect from the nationals.
He will allow that he has something to offer the world,
and will not hide behind the devastating cliche that
"in me dwells no good thing." He will lose none of his
evangelical theology and dedication to Jesus Christ,
but his scope of ministry will be broadened.

We are coming to the place where the missionary profession is held in as high esteem as that of medicine
or science. Thus Missions are having to change in order
to reach the people of the world with all available resources. Many candidates will go to the field as edu-
cators in their field for the specific purpose of teaching nationals how to do the work formerly done by the
foreign missionary, e.g., building mission stations,
manning radio and TV controls, preaching, teaching,
pastoring, nursing, etc. Because candidates today will
follow the advice of D. L. Moody that "it is better to
get 10 men to do the work than to do the work of 10 men",
there will be far more mobility and education in missionary work. The missionary will be willing to give far
more responsibility and authority to nationals and to
train leaders from among them. Trained administrators
will allow decisions to be made on lower levels, thus
conserving time and manpower in field operations. There
will be better use made of available men and women.
Candidates chosen will not be jack-of-all-trades, but
will be prepared for a particular role and sent out for
that specific task.

The people to whom the missionary is being sent are
also in a state of change. They are becoming better edu-

cated and more sophistocated. They are being reached
through literature, radio, television and education
as well as through person-to-person evangelism. They
are beginning to think for themselves and are no
longer satisfied to listen without questioning, or to
believe without reasoning. Young people are caught
up in the maelstrom of radical thinking. They are
learning new methods. They are becoming acquainted
with the outside world.

Thus the missionary image must change. Missions,
themselves, must rethink and plan for the future.
Every man and resource must be used to highest capacity.
Some of the old must make way for the new. Outmoded
methods and operations must be up-dated. Candidates
must be prepared to bridge the gap in this changeover.
The extensive and exciting challenges and opportunities
for creativity and innovation are before you. And
YOU are a vital part of this new look in missions. Are
you prepared for it?

2

Personal Considerations

Although the newly accepted missionary candidate is thinking primarily in terms of "how can I raise my support, when can I leave for the field, where will I buy my equipment, what will I say in my meetings," etc., etc., there is one point that must be kept in mind. The life of a missionary does not begin when one reaches the foreign field. The truth of the matter is, crossing an ocean or a continent has never yet changed a person overnight. It is true that surroundings, language, culture, clothing, food, shelter, and the whole way of life will be different. But the missionary candidate himself is basically the same when he walks up the ramp of the plane in the homeland and when he walks down the ramp on foreign soil.

For some, it is easy to adjust to a new pattern of living. Many find language study very tedious and difficult, or well nigh impossible. Others feel the whole adjustment is interesting and enjoyable. But one thing that does not radically change is *YOU*. And because *YOU* have to live with *YOU* the rest of your life, it is well to consider some of the little things (and big things, too) in your personal life which can be or ought to be adapted, adjusted, deleted or enhanced. And it is never too early to begin! In fact, the earlier you start, the more you'll realize those things that need to be changed in your life to become an effective and stable witness on the field.

The first area to be considered is the PRAYER LIFE.
Do you find it difficult to maintain a Quiet Time?
Have you neglected this vital aspect of your spiritual
life? Have you determined again and again that you
would rise earlier or stay up later to have that time
with the Lord? And have you been pressed from every
side with work and worries and trials and problems so
that you didn't have time for prayer? Have you been
frustrated because you felt a need to pray but didn't
make an opportunity for it? Have you realized a lack
of fruitfulness in your life and through your life to
others because you neglected fellowship with the Lord
through prayer?

Lack of a personal prayer life may be the cause of
more physical, mental and emotional breakdowns than we
would dare to number. It keeps the individual from
finding the working of the Holy Spirit in his life.
Because of unconfessed sin, relationships are severed
with his friends and co-workers, and he soon becomes
self-centered, easily hurt, and gradually he becomes
quite unmanageable for he is working out his own problems and getting himself into precarious situations
when he should be seeking the help of the Lord in all
these matters. "If any of you lack wisdom, let him
ask..."[1] "If ye shall ask anything in my name..."[2]
"Ask and it shall be given you, seek and ye shall find,
knock and it shall be opened unto you..." [3]   "Ye have
not because ye ask not..."[4]

Just like any other part of your spiritual life,
believing God can answer prayer does very little for
you until, by faith, you step out and prove it. And if
you do not have established prayer habits in the homeland, they will be far more difficult to organize on
the mission field. Satan tries even harder to pull you
away from such a ministry when you are in the thick of
the battle.

[1] James 1:5
[2] John 14:14
[3] Matthew 7:7
[4] James 4:2

It is a well-established fact that Amy Carmichael, that great missionary to South India, turned folks away from her door each morning, people whom we might say really needed the help she could have given, people who were hungry and sick and needed spiritual guidance, - and yet Amy Carmichael felt that those morning hours spent in prayer before the Lord were worth far more than the feeble efforts she might have made to care for the needs of others when she had not spent time with her Lord.

The priority of prayer must be established and maintained. It must not become a fanatical type of fetish. (Have you ever known people who had a whole day ruined if for some reason they were not able to spend two hours in prayer at the beginning of the day)? Prayer is not a charm. It is not something you have to do to maintain your salvation. It is not a matter of a short period of "Lord give me this, and Lord give me that." It should be the place of power. It should be like getting your spiritual battery recharged. It should be a time of natural fellowship just as you would spend time talking to, sharing with, and listening to your dearest earthly friend. It should be a joyous time and not something that is dreaded.

If you do not enjoy prayer now, you will enjoy it less on the mission field. If you do not enter wholeheartedly into prayer with others now, you will not be especially keen on sharing others' burdens on the field.

Prayer is an essential part of your ministry. You cannot live or witness without it. So begin *today* if you have not already begun. It is hard work, the mind wanders (praying aloud will help this), and time is at a premium, but prayer is a *must*.

Along with the prayer life must come <u>DAILY BIBLE READING</u>. God's Word is your message. In it are the words of eternal life, and the rules for daily living. It is folly to think that the study of the Word in Bible School is enough to last a lifetime except for following along during the Sunday services. No, the longer you live, the more time you should be spending with the Word. There are some who have chosen as their motto, "No Bible, no breakfast!"

You may not be going to the mission field as a preacher. You may not establish a church or churches, or be involved in a Christian Education ministry. You may not be called upon to oversee a number of national pastors. And yet if your life is to be effective for Christ, and if you are to remain at peace within yourself, you cannot and must not neglect the Word of God.

Families find it more difficult to maintain a time for personal prayer and Bible Reading or for FAMILY FELLOWSHIP than single folks. But it is something that must be established in the home, and it should be done *now*, or it will be doubly hard on the field.

Another matter which must be settled before you proceed to your service is that of GIFTS AND TITHING. Many missionary candidates have the impression that because their support comes from the gifts and tithes of others, there is no need to set a part of this aside specifically for the work of the Lord. But what do we have in life that we have not received from others? No matter what comes into our hands, who it comes from, or how it gets there, we still owe it to the Lord to share it with Him and His work. If you find it difficult to give to the Lord at home, you will find it impossible to give to Him on the field. "But", you say, "isn't it enough that I have given my life to serve on the mission field?" No, it is not! Everything we are and have or ever hope to be must be committed entirely to Him. This includes our pocketbooks. "But when I receive such a little bit, how can I afford to tithe?" The question ought rather to be, "How can I afford *not* to tithe?" Have you discovered the glorious truth that you cannot outgive God? Have you found out for yourself that when you cast your bread upon the waters, it comes back cake with icing? Be sure to give this aspect of your personal life a great deal of consideration now. The Old Testament insisted upon a tenth for the Lord. Should not our gifts and offerings far exceed the letter of the law?

Then there are PERSONAL MATTERS to be settled. Have you ever stopped to ask yourself some of these questions:

Am I hard to get along with?

Do I have a temper?

Do I like to have my own way?

Am I easily hurt?

Do I have feelings of instability?

Do I basically like people and find worth in them?

Do I feel "at home" with people?

Am I concerned about people?

Can I get along well with them?

Have I had good results in witnessing?

Can I effectively deal with adults and children?

Do I love people for themselves or only because of their spiritual condition?

Do I have a good sense of humor?

Can I laugh at myself, or only at the expense of others?

Is there anyone or anything that takes precedence over God in my life?

Do I find it difficult to apologize?

Do I have a sense of perspective?

Do I stick to a job until it's finished?

Do I work well with others and share the credit with them?

Am I considerate of others?

Do I worry and fret over insignificant problems?

Do I make allowances for mistakes in others?

Is my way the only way a thing should be done?

Am I generous?

Am I given to hospitality?

Am I jealous?

Am I a good listener?

How do I handle gossip?

Can I follow or do I always have to be the leader?

Am I grateful or do I expect to receive more than I give?

How do I get along on a limited budget?

How do I react to sickness in myself and in others?

What do I consider the necessities of life?

How do I see and accept myself and my abilities?

Am I forgiving?

Does my life genuinely show forth the fruit of the Spirit?

Although you cannot of and by yourself change your whole personality, there are areas which you can attempt to improve.

Perhaps even more to the point we might ask: What is my real motive for going to the mission field? Does my church expect it of me? Has my family pushed me into it? Am I trying to get away from an unpleasant situation at home? Is it an adventure? Do I have the feeling I can change the course of the universe? Do I feel it's my duty to go? Am I going because my life's partner feels called? Or am I going because of my deep love and concern for the people to whom I'm going, because God has unmistakeably called me, personally, and because I am equipped to do something for the spiritual condition of those to whom I am going?

When you arrive on the field, Satan will try to question you over and over again why you are there, what you are accomplishing, and why you don't give up and go home. You must have an answer that will satisfy you and will turn away Satan at times like that. Therefore, you must carefully consider before you ever leave the homeland what your motives are for going, and then plan what your goals will be for staying.

You must never allow your mind to stagnate. Saturate it with good reading material. Keep posted concerning events in the country to which you will eventually go, and keep abreast of work in other fields. Find out what methods are being used and whether or not they are working. Seek out books which give the background and history of your people. Attend conferences and workshops which will keep you up-to-date on trends in the world of missions. If you are not interested in learning at home, you will not begin on the field.

YOU ARE A MISSIONARY TODAY. What you are today will determine largely what you will be tomorrow. And what you are at home will determine mainly what you will be on the mission field. Are you content with your life as it is? Or are there some changes and improvements which you want to make to help smooth the pathway of your missionary career?

3

Preparation For Service

Following Acceptance

Candidates who will be engaged primarily in teaching the Word, evangelizing, setting up Christian Education programs among nationals, teaching in Bible Institutes and Short Term Bible Schools, coordinating the churches in one or more areas, supervising national pastors, and preaching ministries will, ordinarily, be required to obtain Bible College and/or Seminary training in the homeland before acceptance. Candidates who will engage in specific ministries associated with medicine, secretarial work, teaching, engineering, photography, administration, etc., should have a good background in Bible knowledge (formal or informal) and preferably a degree in their particular specialty. Missionaries should be among the best trained individuals in the world. Your Mission Board will, of course, set the educational standards for your ministry.

Apart from formal education, it should be the desire of those facing the field to become thoroughly acquainted with their Mission Board, its background, its history, its progress, where it works, who works under its auspices, its affiliation with other Christian groups, how it functions, what its policies and procedures are, what its requirements are, how much authority the leadership assumes, what part the missionary plays in the carrying forward of the administrative aspects of the work, what the support level is, what kind of schooling is available for children, benefits, retirement, insurance, health expenses. You cannot know your Mission Board too well! Study it and be satisfied that you can work within its framework without stress, making a contribution, not criticizing, being proud of the work and the workers. Remember that no mission board is entirely perfect, and even if it were, it would cease to be so when you joined it!

Reading missionary biographies and literature is excellent preparation for what lies ahead. Much can be learned from the work of others. This is what must be built upon. Knowing where others succeeded and failed can be of tremendous importance. The life stories of God's servants are stimulating, challenging and encouraging.

Bible and Missionary Conferences should be attended, not just with the idea in mind that you may be asked to speak and thereby support could be raised. It is very possible that this may be the case, but first and foremost, attend seeking the Lord's blessing for your own life, being fueled for the flight into an unknown pathway, being strengthened in the inner man by the Word and power of God, and becoming excited about the opportunities for witness and the wide open doors for the Gospel to be preached in this day. You may listen to missionaries from the area to which you are assigned. You may also hear from those who are working in the homeland. It is good to hear these reports and to be reminded once again that the field is the world, and the work of a missionary is far more a vocation than a location.

You would benefit from availing yourself of the opportunity to take a correspondence course in Bible and/or in your specialty just to keep your mind and knowledge up-to-date on these matters, to learn modern methods and procedures, and new ways of presenting old truths.

There are many short specialty courses available in most areas. A secretary may wish to brush up on short-hand, typing or bookkeeping at a local Business School; a nurse or doctor may have opportunity to attend work-shops and seminars to increase knowledge and skills. Hospitals are sometimes willing to allow medical per-sonnel the privilege of attending special courses to give them further ability and training in specific areas.

Industrial experience or work in a secular setting may also be of help to some workers. Some missions require their engineers to work for a year or two in industry before going to the field, and other professional people have also benefited from this type of training.

Learn about magazines which are available in your specialty and be sure these are ordered so you can keep in step with your profession while you are out of the homeland. You will be amazed at the rapidity with which things change!

If you have children, get them interested in reading missionary books, or if they are younger, read missionary stories to them and try to explain about the location and probable living conditions of the country to which you are assigned.

Visit several organizations in the homeland to compare procedures and sources of information and methods of doing your particular job. If you are a doctor, visit several hospitals, ask questions, look at equipment; as a secretary, find out the latest and best office procedures, learn about machines available, do some cost analyses; make recommendations to your Board about equipment which you feel might make a contribution to the work (if it is not already available on the field). Be a detective!

Develop a sense of mental alertness, keenness and observation. Learn some manual skills. You may have to be a fix-it man (even if you happen to be a single girl). Take up a satisfying hobby such as wood carving, sewing, stamp collecting, art, music, or any one of a hundred other things. Learn to play with people. Be a good sport. Take up sports. You will have times on the field when you will need the mental, physical and emotional recreation and stimulus which comes from play and laughter. Learn how to relax and how to help others to do so. It is good therapy.

Learn to live with nervous tension and frustrations. How do you fare when your privacy is denied? How do you face loneliness? Find the answers. Be cheerful, patient. Humor is an essential part of missionary life. The best humor is to laugh at yourself and your own mistakes. Humor should never be aimed against your fellow missionaries or nationals. That is not humor at all. Develop vision. Don't live with blinders on. See your problems and your joys and your corner of the world as only one little part of a gigantic whole. Give encouragement to those who are doing a hard job well. Develop gratefulness and appreciation. Never forget Christian and common courtesy. Learn to give cheerfully of your time and of yourself. Don't take anyone for granted. Don't look down on people. Don't degrade yourself. Be strictly honest with yourself and others. You are, in truth, an Ambassador for the King of kings. The more you learn at home, the easier it will be for you on the field.

Become acquainted with Church History. Be sure you know your own Mission's policy regarding the establishment of churches and the way they are to be governed. You may be taking over a church previously administered by another denominational group. Making a Church of England a Baptist Church as soon as you arrive can be confusing to the nationals and devastating to the work.

Seriously consider the adviseability of taking further studies before you leave for the field. Many a nurse has realized, after being on the field for a few months, that she would have done well to get her Bachelor's or Master's degree in order to carry out her role properly. Other professional people may feel likewise. Even though it will delay your going to the field for another one or two years, it is far more practical to get your education now than to try to cram it into your furlough time, or have to ask for an extension of furlough or leave of absence in order to obtain a further degree. Inquire of your mission board as to where they expect you will be utilized in the overall sphere of your specialization. It it is in any type of supervisory or teaching capacity, question the possibility and feasibility of more training.

4

Arranging Deputation Meetings

Immediately following your acceptance by your Board, you will want to begin lining up friends and meetings in order to present your testimony and the work in which you will be engaged. Even though you may have another year of Bible School, work experience, professional training, college or Graduate School, it is best to get started with deputation immediately. This not only gives you a longer time to make yourself known to friends and churches, but as funds come into your account, it helps with the outgoing expenses which, of necessity, cause a heavy drain on your account at the time you leave for your field of service. It also helps you to get involved in the work of being a missionary right where you are, and keeps you enthusiastic about your future ministry as you share it with others.

The most practical place to begin asking for deputation meetings and speaking engagements is in your home church, in the churches of your closest friends, and where you are known best. Although in many ways, your home area is the hardest place you will ever have to speak, it is a place where you will often find folks sympathetic to your calling and ambition. It is at least a starting place to get your feet off the ground in this difficult, yet joyous and rewarding task of deputation.

But where do you go from your home church? Or perhaps your home church does not favor your decision. Or you, as a member of a Faith Mission Board cannot be supported by your denominational church. How do you find opportunities to present your work?

Let's list a few possible areas where meetings may be obtained:

1. Your pastor may have friends who would be willing to give you a hearing in their congregations.

2. If there is an Evangelical Ministers' Association in your area, contact the pastors within this group.

3. Your Bible College Alumni Association will have a list of pastors available for you to contact in any area you request.

4. Friends in other areas may invite you to their church or school.

5. Never overlook the possibility of radio and television interviews.

6. Rotary Club, Girl Scouts, Boy Scouts, Lions Club and other Civic and Social groups may ask you to speak. Additional contacts are usually made through these channels.

7. You may be invited to present a class in a school on the history, geography, or culture of the country to which you are going.

8. Meetings are often held in homes where interested folks gather in a small group to hear you. You could invite them to your home, or suggest having a meeting in theirs.

9. Many camps and conferences utilize missionary speakers during the summer, and are willing to make a project of giving to a missionary candidate.

10. Daily Vacation Bible Schools may be willing to present you as their missionary project.

11. Become aware of missionary conferences to be held in churches in your area. Present yourself to these churches. Many times they are seeking those whom they can support. And if they do not pledge financial support, often much prayer support is gained.

12. If your mission has deputation representatives, or regional representatives, be sure to contact them for meetings when you are to be in their area.

13. Even if your Board does not have Representatives appointed to help with your deputational contacts, it is very possible they would share with you the names of churches from their mailing and donor lists.

14. Obtain telephone directories from your local phone company for cities and towns you wish to visit. The yellow pages will list the churches in the area.

15. City and large town newspapers usually carry a church page once each week, and smaller town papers will carry this in their weekly issue. Churches in the area are usually listed.

16. Denominational groups often support faith missionaries. Request a copy of the denominational yearbook. This will give you the name and address and pastor of each church within that denominational group.

17. Home Bible Study classes and prayer groups.

18. Bible College Prayer Bands.

19. Youth for Christ, Keen Teen, Youthtime and other regularly scheduled youth rallies.

After obtaining the names of churches and groups that might be interested in utilizing you in a meeting, write a personal letter to each one asking if there is a possibility that you could present your testimony and your work at their convenience or when it would be mutually

convenient.   If you must send a form letter, be sure
to include at least a short personal note at the close.

This letter should include the following information:

1.   Your full name and where you can be reached.

2.   The types of meetings at which you are pre-
pared to speak (Morning service, Evening ser-
vice, Mid-week prayer meeting, Ladies' Meeting,
Men's Club, Sunday School, Childrens' Churches,
Junior or Senior High Young People, Boys'
Brigade, Pioneer Girls, etc.)

3.   Give complete details concerning what you plan
to present in the meeting.

4.   If you have slides, tapes, films, visual aids,
literature, posters, displays, curios, or
other "props", be sure to mention what is
available and ask what they might like for you
to arrange to use.

5.   Offer at least two dates when you would be
available to speak.

6.   Be sure to give information concerning the
Mission to which you belong, where you expect
to serve, and what type of work you will be
doing.   (Some work has more appeal to one church
or group or area than another).

7.   Enclose a piece of general literature from your
mission.

Always enclose a stamped self-addressed envelope
with your letter of request.   Use Mission letterhead
stationery if it is available to you.   This makes your
request more "official".

It is often true that you receive surprisingly few
responses.   Don't become discouraged with this.   No
matter how few places you may speak, or how few people
may attend the meeting, BE ENTHUSIASTIC.   And keep con-
tacting other groups.   You will be encouraged, too, to
receive requests from groups.   Some candidates are

requested by so many that outgoing support and expenses
are raised with very little correspondence being necessary
Do not, however, just sit back and expect invitations
to come to you. Diligently seek them out.

After you have received word from a church, group,
or individual concerning a meeting date, be sure to
acknowledge this promptly in writing and reveal definite
plans.

Unless absolutely essential, never turn away an
opportunity to present the work of your ministry to a
group of people interested enough to invite you. You
will be amazed and thrilled to see where God has placed
His people. YOUR SUPPORT WILL USUALLY COME FROM THE
MOST UNEXPECTED PLACES. Friends and churches you had
depended upon may not be the source of God's supply
for you.

As much as possible, work in one geographical area
at a time. Cross-country hops are both time and money
consuming. Unless especially invited by those who
offer support beforehand, pray earnestly before travel-
ling great distances (over 500 miles) for a single
meeting.

As you build up a list of interested friends, they
will, normally, form four distinct categories:

1. An inner circle of prayer supporters (those
    with whom you will share problems and joys
    in a personal way).

2. Financial supporters (those who will pledge
    monthly or annual support).

3. Those who have a general interest in you.

4. Those who have a general interest in your
    Mission Board.

Some of these categories may overlap, of course.

There is a possibility that you could volunteer your
services in local churches, helping in DVBS, teaching
in Sunday School, organizing a visitation program or

assisting the pastor. In this way you would become
known by these people and you would be able to minister
to their spiritual needs. But do not offer such assistance to a body of believers with the sole hope of
gaining financial support from them.

Some of you may be in an internship program and
have already been promised your support by a church.
Or your home church may have promised to supply your
needs. It is still essential for you to speak to other
groups and gain their interest in you and your work.
Again, consider it a ministry to them and a privilege
to have them share your prayer burdens. Don't deny them
the possibility of having a part in your work. Also, if
you are supported by individuals in a church, there is
a possibility that you may need help from others in the
future. An additional child in the family, the death
of a supporter, or an increase in field allowance will
mean more funds will be needed. The more widely you
are known and prayed for, the more concern they will
have for you when you face additional needs.

5

Preparing For
And Presenting Your Meetings

There will come a day when you receive an invitation to speak at your first deputational meeting. It will come with mixed emotion. You will be glad for the opportunity, and you will be wondering what to say and do.

First of all, there are several things you should NOT do:

. . . Do not give a Bible study

. . . Do not preach

. . . Do not try to be something you are not

. . . Do not run down other missions or missionaries

. . . Do not try to tell everything you know

. . . Do not give the impression you have given up everything worthwhile in life in order to become a missionary

. . . Do not be apologetic in your approach

If you are speaking in a church that knows you well and has been following the Lord's leading in your life, it may not be necessary to give your experience concerning your "call" to missionary service. But in places

where you are not so well known, the best way to acquaint
people with you and your work is by way of your personal
testimony.

Since, in most cases, you have not visited your
field of service, you will not be able to give detailed
reports of that which is happening on the field. You
cannot show your personal slides of your work. You can
merely quote facts and stories which have come down to
you from someone else. Although these can be used very
effectively by some people, others are not at all good
along this line.

But a personal testimony is your very own. No one
can give or take this from you. It is a way of sharing
the Lord with others, and giving an opportunity to folks
to see that the Lord has led you step by step. And it
allows you the privilege of communicating your salvation
experience to English-speaking people before you have to
do the more difficult task of getting this witness to
people of a different language.

Perhaps your mission has loaned you a set of slides,
or a film depicting the work to which you will be going.
A friend in the mission may have loaned you pictures.
Or you may have been a short-term worker on the field
and have your own slides. Be sure, at any rate, that
you understand the work which is presented in this way.
Make sure you can answer questions which may be raised
from such a presentation. Know the names of the missionary personnel with whom you will be serving.

Preparation is your key to success. It is easy to
think that giving your testimony requires no prior consideration. This is not true. Although a testimony
belongs to you, and you alone, it is not merely a
recital of "I did this, I did that, I went here, I went
there, and all of a sudden here I am going to the
mission field." A testimony is far more than a life
history. It is, in fact, a Psalm of praise and a witness to the fact of God's working in your life. It is
not YOU at all, but HIM. It is not a false pretense
of attributing to Him what you have done, but a life
lived so completely in harmony with Him that unknowingly
it has been His life lived through you. Your testimony
must never leave people feeling sorry for you, or stir

people in such a way that they remember only an emotion.
It must direct the hearer to the Lord Jesus Christ and
what He is able to do in a life that is committed to
Him.   People WILL remember you, but always they should
be pointed to the Savior.

Many missionary candidates miss out on opportunities
for soul winning in their deputation meetings because
they focus attention on themselves rather than on the
Lord. A true testimony not only shares what Christ has
done for you, but what He can do for each one who is
present in the meeting. Missionary work begins in your
very first meeting. Don't miss out on these occasions
by presenting yourself instead of the Lord. And yet
remember - DON'T PREACH UNLESS YOU'VE BEEN ASKED!

With these things in mind, be sure to plan for
every minute of your first meeting. If you are allowed
to speak 30 minutes, plan for 29 and be through in 29!
This will please both pastor and people and may provide an opportunity for a return visit. NEVER RUN OVER
THE TIME ALLOTTED TO YOU. Have a goal when you speak.
Don't cover everything in one meeting.

Preparing for a 30-minute presentation is not nearly
so difficult as preparing for a 5-minute spot. Never
despise the little time given to you. But be sure you
have in mind exactly what you want to give and how you
are going to present it. To be sure, you cannot give
your testimony, a history of your mission, tell what
you will be doing on the field, and be assured that
people will take in all that you say. But dwell on one
fact. Make sure this one aspect is clearly in the minds
of your listeners when you are through.

If you have planned on a 15-minute film or slide
presentation in the 30 minutes available to you, be absolutely certain that you have an alternate 15-minute
presentation to fill this spot in the event that the
lights should fail, the projector jams, or your bulb
burns out. Such situations can be disastrous if you do
not have an alternate plan.

Humor is not out of place on the platform. Illustrations have their place, also. It is true, however,
that people will sometimes leave a meeting remembering

only a joke that was told, or a cute story which illus-
trated your main point, and for the very life of them
they can remember little else of what you have tried to
get across to them.

Be spontaneous in your presentation. NEVER READ
YOUR TESTIMONY. If you have notes, be sure to refer
to them sparingly, and do be careful not to spill them
on the floor!

Each time you speak you should say things in a
different way. Don't become stereotyped. Don't speak
by rote. Be enthusiastic. Your own enthusiasm will,
many times, determine the response of your congregation.
We hear much about the "enthusiasm of youth". Older
folks warm up to this type of presentation. It takes
them back to the days when they, too, were "on fire"
for the Lord and His work. Many of them may have
cooled off through the years, and your presence may well
be the spark that ignites them to once again serve the
Lord with vigor. (And what pastor wouldn't be pleased
to have ten people become enthused about teaching Sunday
School, or providing transportation for DVBS, or praying,
or volunteering for work in Pioneer Girls, Awana Club or
the Church Library)? Just make sure that your enthusiasm
is based on reality, and not just something you have
manufactured along the way. If the work to which you
have been called does not thrill you, perhaps you need
to reconsider your call, or at least your attitude
toward it.

There are other things which you may want to take
into consideration as you prepare for those first meetings. Are you musical? Perhaps you will want to provide
a musical selection during the time allotted to you.
Are you a chalk artist? It might be good to illustrate
your talk, or provide a short sample of what you expect
to be doing on the field.

Of course you will take into consideration the group
of people to whom you are speaking. Your presentation
to a Junior Church group might differ considerably from
that given to an adult prayer meeting.

For some of you, the very thought of deputation meetings will be almost more than you can bear. Being shy

by nature, introvertive, not used to speaking in public,
insecure -- the task looks gigantic and impossible.
Perhaps you are going to the field as an engineer,
secretary or mechanic. You may think that people will
not be as interested in you as they are in those who
are going to work in a hospital, an orphanage, or in
"down-country" village evangelism. But YOU ARE THE ONE
WHO CAN MAKE THE DIFFERENCE. Be yourself. Exalt the
Lord. And "with God, nothing is impossible". (And if
it is any encouragement to you, sometimes the poorest
platform personnel are really the best missionaries).
Don't despair. Don't give up before you begin. Don't
let your enthusiasm wane. God has given you a job to
do which cannot be done by anyone else. Is this not
sufficient cause for sharing it, even if the words
come haltingly?

Along with a very thorough preparation for your
first meetings is the most important ingredient for
your presentation. We are speaking of PRAYERparation.
Time spent in prayer is never wasted. Dependence upon
Him, and gratefulness to Him can tremendously magnify
the effectiveness of your presentation. Commit your
way unto Him, and He WILL bring it to pass. He WILL
guide you with His eye as you look "full in His wonderful face". Prayer not only makes your presentation
effective, but it can pave the way for the working of
the Spirit of God in your meetings.

In the case of married couples and those with families, it must be decided whether both you and your wife
will speak during the time allotted to you, or if one
of you will do the speaking for the family. It will
depend upon whether you are to have one meeting at a
given group or church, or if there will be other opportunities. Some folks have found it effective to intro-
duce their children in the meeting, and if a musical
team can be formed, a song sung in the language of the
people to whom you are going can be most effective. But
NEVER FORCE YOUR CHILDREN TO PERFORM IN PUBLIC.

Be prepared for the unexpected. You must always
have a back-up program for your services. And you must
have a few extra messages up your sleeve, for you will
often be asked to speak at several meetings rather than
just the one you were engaged for. Or perhaps there are

several speakers and when they get to you, your time has diminished from 15 minutes to 2 minutes! You will surely panic in such a situation if you have never thought of the possibility of it.

Preparation should take into consideration this important fact: Not only should you tell people what YOU want them to know. Be sure you tell them what THEY want to know.

In many churches you will be "competing" with other missionaries for a hearing, either those already supported by the church, or other candidates passing through. Only by "being yourself" and presenting an honest picture can you hope that the group will remember you.

Be sure to have your own projection equipment available in case the church is not prepared for you. Plan to arrive at least 15 minutes before meeting time. If your family will be with you, be sure to inform the church in the event they want to provide meals and /or accommodations. (Always indicate the ages and sex of the children). Plan how you will set up your display table and request this facility in your correspondence.

Occasionally you will run into a church which has split or is having inner disputes. Stay absolutely neutral in these situations. Do not side with factions. Do not talk about other members of the congregation. Do not become involved in church difficulties.

Many Mission Boards request that financial needs NOT be mentioned in public. You will, however, find that people will ask you specific questions. These should be answered as thoroughly and candidly as the person desires. Money cannot be ignored. Outright advertising of specific needs, however, may be against the policies of your Board. Be sure to clarify this point with your Home Office.

Always be courteous and considerate in the homes where you are entertained. Don't impose on your host or hostess. Offer to help with their work. Send a note of appreciation to all who have provided hospitality for you.

The prayer support obtained during your ministry is essential. Some groups will pray; others will give financially. Both are needed.

Deputation work is not merely a matter of speaking in a great number of churches to try to raise funds to build up your account. Each individual contact is important. Be interested in the people and their outreach and ministry. Never act as though you have come to give sacrificial service just to obtain an offering. If this is your goal, you will not be blessed or be a blessing in your ministry.

6

The Prayer
Or Newsletter/Circular

The term "Prayer Letter" was apparently coined to
designate form letters sent out by missionaries in
which various facts were mentioned as prayer items on
the part of those who received this correspondence.
Perhaps the broader term, "Newsletter" would be more
appropriate today since most missionaries try to give
items of interest about their field and their work
and their family along with definite requests for
prayer and praise. This does not take away from the
importance of prayer, but rather gives those on your
mailing list a more "in-depth" look at your work so
that they might catch a bit of the flavor of your
ministry, and thus be able to pray even more effectively
for the requests that you will bring before them. Your
first letter will probably be sent at the time of your
acceptance for missionary service.

The simplest, and LEAST personal way of keeping in
touch with folks is by means of the periodic printed
letter. Even so, it is a necessity to get this word
into the hands of those who are interested in you. It
should be as personal as you can make it, for in many
cases, it will take the place of the personal letter
you do not or cannot write.

The following matters should be determined before
you sit down to write your prayer letters:

1. What should be included in the letter?

2. How often should it be sent?

3. To whom should it be sent?

4. What should it accomplish?

5. Why is it important?

6. What format should I use?

Set goals for your letters. Aim for a unity through-out. Make your letters unique. Make them attractive. Make them meaningful. Avoid vague and general state-ments and the use of foreign words unless pertinent and interpreted. Make them concise. Be careful of grammar and spelling. Use pictures, maps, illustrations and/or line drawings where feasible. Determine whether or not you will send them to unsaved friends.

Your letter should be something that your friends, supporters and acquaintances will look forward to re-ceiving. People are far too busy to wade through two or three pages of material which is so full of meat that it hardly contains paragraphs. Condense your material into bite-size pieces. Line drawings can often produce more of an impact than a full page of solid print. A photograph in print gives impact to what you write. Be sure to leave plenty of "white space" on your letter. Use word pictures so the reader can "see" where you are and what you are doing. Try to avoid typographical errors. If at all possible, have your letters printed (offset press) or mimeographed. Too many times a hecto-graphed letter is not readable.

Avoid beginning your letter with a verse of Scripture. The unsaved are not interested. The saved pass over it, assuming they know it already. Scripture verses may be utilized in the body of the letter as necessary.

Rather than a normal letter-like circular, you might want to use a newspaper style with various headings or a journal, or a diary. In some cases a letter within an outline is very effective. (The map of Africa or South America, for example, is excellent for this type of pre-sentation). Or for special letters you may want to write in the shape of a Christmas tree, cross, wedding bell, or heart.

Remember that before any of the material you have labored long hours to produce has been read, the appearance of your letter will determine its effectiveness.

You are not limited to black print on white paper. Colored stock makes a better impression with people than white even though the cost may be slightly higher. Use a good quality of paper. If you are mimeographing both sides of a sheet, use a heavy enough paper so that the print doesn't show through.

Your letters are not for the purpose of preaching a sermon. This can be done in personal letters if you feel led to do so. But the prayer or newsletter should contain information concerning you, your mission, your work, and the part that those who receive your letters can have in your ministry by prayer.

When you mention prayer requests, especially specific prayer for meetings or special campaigns, exams, or definite events, be sure that those dates are still pertinent by the time your people receive the letters. There is nothing more frustrating than being asked to pray for a meeting that was held the previous month.

Don't let your letters sound like a mimeographed form letter! Make them personal and intimate, as though each one of your readers were the only one receiving the letter. To make them even more personal, add a handwritten note to each one, or at least sign them personally (unless an individual or a church has volunteered to send them out for you). Occasionally give information as to where changes of address can be sent. Whenever it is humanly possible, it is best for you to send your letters personally. Even when you are on the field this is a good practice if the regulations of the country in which you find yourself allow you to do so.

As a point of interest, if you plan to send your prayer letters from the field, be sure to use a stamp or stamps from your country on the envelope. There is nothing more devastating than to receive a letter from a foreign country that has been run through a stamp machine, especially if the individual is an avid stamp collector. A real stamp on the envelope sets your letter apart from others and makes it unique. It is a curiosity arouser, and thus it stands to reason that the addressee will be more apt to open the flap and pull out the letter. If he's gotten that far, it's a cinch that he will open the letter and at least glance through it. And if you have made your letter attractive and readable, he will take the time to enjoy it, and, in fact, will look forward to receiving the next one. This is true of letters mailed in the homeland, also. Use commemorative stamps rather than ordinary postage or machine stamps.

A family picture should be included at least once a year. You know how quickly the children change, and how anxious everyone is to see that the mission field has not drawn away every ounce of physical beauty and stamina from you! For single folks, it is always well to include a picture of yourself in some aspect of your work at least once a year also.

Less than three or four prayer letters sent each year cannot keep the interest of people focused on you. Keep in mind for future reference that a small token souvenir enclosed in your letter sent from the field will produce far more interest than you can imagine. Send a snapshot, bookmark, clipping from your local newspaper in the national language, or a few cancelled stamps. Inexpensive, but thoughtful.

How do you build up your letter list? This will vary with individual preference. Some missionaries send a newsletter to every friend, relative, and acquaintance with whom they come into contact. Others send only a few letters, just to supporting churches and individuals. There are several ways of building your list:

1. Close family friends and relatives

2. Obtain lists of individuals in your home church who want to receive your news

3. When in new churches, leave mimeographed request sheets on the display or literature table, mention them, and allow people to sign up to receive your letters

4. Announce in your meetings that if folks want your letter, they should speak to you personally

5. In supporting churches, ask the pastor how many copies he feels can be prayerfully utilized. These can be sent bulk rate in care of the pastor

6. Prayer Bands at Bible Schools and Colleges

7. Home Bible Study and Prayer groups

At least once every two years, send a card asking people to return it if they want to remain on your list. DON'T OBLIGATE PEOPLE TO RECEIVE YOUR LETTERS. Give them this opportunity to be removed from your list.

Be sure to put your FULL name and address and your mission name and address on the bottom of each letter.

If a friend or organization in the homeland is going to send out your letters, be sure they keep you informed of address changes. You should have an up-to-date list in your possession at all times. It is preferable to send letters by first class mail, but this will depend upon the size of your mailing list and the amount of financial burden you can underwrite for this project.

Always send a copy of your finished letter to the Home Office. Some Boards will require you to have your letter o.k.'d by them before you are allowed to mail it. The Home Director or Field Director is responsible for this detail in most cases. Check with your Home Office concerning specific regulations in this regard.

Usually your Home Office is not equipped to handle the mailing of your newsletters. They would, however, be appreciative of names and addresses of those from your list who might like to receive general mailings from the mission.

Try to confine your letter to one page. Long letters lose readers.

Newsletters are usually a personal expense or work support item. There is a great deal of work involved in getting out a mailing. Unless you are paying an organization to do this for you, be sure to send a word of special appreciation to the church or friends who may be carrying on this ministry for you each time a letter goes out.

7

Prayer Cards

A picture is worth far more than words. Those who have met you recently, those who may have been impressed during your one meeting in their church, those who are most apt to forget you because they know you the least -- these are the ones who will appreciate having a reminder of the one for whom they are praying and in whom they are interested.

Although some missionary candidates feel that much money is wasted on prayer cards, it would seem that this is not accurate. It is true that many prayer cards are disposed of in various ways, either immediately upon arrival in a strange home, or shortly thereafter. But if only one in ten, or one in twenty produces a more sincere prayer burden for you, it is an inexpensive piece of literature.

How do you go about preparing the prayer card? First of all, let's consider the essential items that MUST be included on it:

1. Your picture

2. Your name

3. Your address (either home or field)

4. The Mission's name

5. The Mission's address

6. Where you will be serving

Other factors are entirely up to you. For example:

1. Do you want a family picture?

2. Do you want to include the names of the children?

3. Do you want to include a map?

4. Do you want to use a line sketch drawing which will indicate at a glance the type of ministry in which you will be engaged?

5. Do you want the card printed in one color, two colors, full color?

6. Would you prefer to use colored stock with black ink?

7. Do you want white stock with black or colored ink?

8. Do you want heavy stock, light stock, coated stock?

9. Do you want a wallet size, bookmark type, folder (2 or 3-fold), special cut (e.g. nurses cap, praying hands), formal invitation type, flat type with no flaps, printed on one side or both?

10. Do you want to include a Scripture verse?

11. How much can you plan to spend for these cards?

12. Where will they be printed?

Your prayer card should identify YOU and YOUR ministry. It should not be so large that it will not fit in a Bible, or on a map of the world. It should not be so small that it will become easily misplaced. It should not be gaudy, but in good taste, and colorful enough and attractive enough to be a true prayer reminder. It should be distinct. It must be printed well.

Before designing your layout, art work and color, set down on paper, or in your mind, the goals you want to reach by distribution of these reminders. Once you have decided these basic factors, locate a printer who is willing to help you choose the card which will be best suited to your particular needs. After you have outlined to the printer (or the artist, if you have opportunity to work through a professional) just what you want your card to communicate, be sure to determine approximately how many cards you will want printed. Always insist on the highest quality of work.

The next question is the matter of distributing these cards.

Again, this is a personal choice and there is no "right" way of distribution. There are many ways, however, in which these cards may be used:

1. You may want to enclose one in a letter telling of your acceptance for missionary service.

2. You may wish to put them on a literature table at your deputation meetings and let individuals take one if they desire.

3. You may have a sign-up sheet at the back of the church so that if a prayer card is wanted, you will have the opportunity of sending one in the mail at a later date. (This, of course, serves the purpose of renewing a contact with a very casual acquaintance).

4. You may want to wait until your second or third newsletter before sending a card to your mailing list.

5. You may want to enclose a card with each letter you send to churches requesting meetings.

6. You may choose to enclose one with each thank-you letter written to those who contribute to your account at meetings.

7. Churches where you have spoken may request a quantity for distribution.

8.   You might ask your pastor if you could enclose
     them in each bulletin on a given Sunday.

9.   You may decide to give them only to your
     supporters.

10. You might want to send them to arrive with a
     letter telling of your departure date.

The old saying, "out of sight, out of mind" can be
very true in missionary life. As you travel from
church to church and home to home, people will appear
very interested in you and your work and your field.
But a year later, when several others like you have
passed through, there will come a numbness of memory concerning you. A pictorial reminder which has been slipped
into a Bible, tacked on a wall, or placed on the mantel
will, in a moment, bring back clear memories of you and
your visit. It is a silent, yet forceful reminder of
you and your ministry.

For some candidates, the prayer card will be a personal expense item. Others will be able to charge it to
their mission account. In some cases, a friend will volunteer payment for them. Sometimes a printer will donate
his services as a personal ministry. But whatever the
case, it is important that you put into the hands of those
who are interested in you the information which will
help them to remember you. And perhaps the most vital
and personal reminder is your prayer card.

8

Preparing A Display

Many times, especially if you are invited to
a missionary conference, the inviting church will request that you set up a display depicting your field
of service or area of work. In a day when people are
used to high quality and technical work, it is imperative that your display be both exceedingly attractive and tell exactly what you want it to say about
yourself, your mission, your work, your field, or
whichever point you want to emphasize. In some instances, your Board will have had some excellent
displays prepared by professionals which are available to you whenever needed. Be sure to notify the
Board well in advance, giving complete details concerning the place and date of your meeting and when
you want the display to arrive.

But not all missionaries have the Home Office on
which to fall back. Most Boards feel that displays
are expensive, difficult to keep in circulation and
unwieldy to manage. Thus you will be forced to use
your own creativity or obtain the help of a friend in
planning your own.

Try to remember that you may be speaking at a
large conference for a week with 60 other missionaries
who have set up 25 or 30 displays. You are competing
for attention. Make your display say something, do
something and be something very special. Perhaps you
can get ideas from TV ads. You may attend a convention
where professionals are displaying their goods. You

may get ideas directly from a newspaper, or from your
local grocery store, or from a window while you are
shopping. Displays are more common today than ever before. Everywhere you look you can pick up ideas for
an effective visual presentation.

Perhaps you will want to use a continuous film or
slide series as your main focus. You may wish to use
pictures (5" x 7" or 8" x 10" in color, if at all possible)
as your background. Captions should be short, meaningful,
and easy to read. Mission literature can be placed in
the foreground. Always have literature available, but
NEVER call a literature table a display! A pad and pen-
cil may be necessary so passersby can sign up for your
prayer card, prayer letter, or to be put on your mission
mailing list.

You may want to use a map of your country as a back-
drop. It should be outlined in black and your area of
service should be circled if you have been assigned to
a definite station or area.

Curios may be utilized to good advantage in your
display. A leopard skin, Japanese lantern, national
newspaper -- you will think of dozens of items which can
lend color and meaning to your display. Books and/or
records may also be available.

A display is a unique program geared to telling a
complete story. It will probably be manned by you or
a member of your mission, but in the event it is not,
it should speak for itself and answer questions through
visual presentation.

When you are asked to provide a display, be sure to
ask how much space will be available to you, if you will
have a table provided, if there will be space at the
rear and sides and if backing wood or cardboard will be
provided to assist in this regard, if cloth or corru-
gated paper will be available, if you need to carry your
own cloth, nails, hammer, ruler, and other equipment, if
there is an electrical outlet available at the site
of your display, if extension cords will be needed, if
anyone will be sharing this area with you, if someone
will be available to help at the particular time you
will be working on your display. Be sure to find out

when time has been set aside for the setting up of
displays and when they will be open to the public.

Your display is another extension of you and your
Board. Strangely enough, people will be far more
attracted to both if they appreciate your display.
Your efforts will be well rewarded, and at each conference you will probably pick up good ideas from
others to incorporate in your future displays.

9

Outfit And Equipment

From the time you receive word of your acceptance for missionary service until the day you actually leave for the field, you will be faced with the question of what to take with you. At one time it was necessary to take not only those things that would make life normally comfortable, but also the bare necessities. Although there may be some corners of the earth where essentials are still not available, for the most part you will not need to load yourself down with food items, toilet tissue, soap, tin bathtubs, and other such niceties.

Normal questions are posed by the candidate:

...Are there items which the government of the country to which I am going prohibits my taking with me?

...On what items are customs duty excessive?

...How much clothing do I need to take?

...Should I take appliances?

...What about wedding gifts, i.e., good china, sterling, crystal?

...Will they have shoes to fit me?

...How much will it cost me to ship my unaccompanied baggage by ship or by air?

...If I don't take everything with me, are packages allowed to be sent to me later?

...What about a car or truck?

...Should I take a gun?

...Will I need special permits for any items?

There are no uniform answers to these questions. Your Mission will provide a general listing of items which you may wish to take with you. This may be broken down into two or three categories listing essentials, those things which are optional, and those things which are handy to have but would be considered "luxuries".

It is always a good idea to correspond with one or more folks who have been stationed on your field for a number of years. They will know the things which are now available in the country, whether these will serve your purpose, whether it would be less expensive to buy them in the homeland and ship them rather than purchasing them at a higher price on your station, those things which should definitely be included in your equipment, types of clothing which are most practical, or taboo. You will find out what the temperature and weather is like in your assigned field. It makes a world of difference whether it will be cold or hot, damp or dry, urban or rural. You may be on the equator, but if you are 10,000 feet above sea level, the weather will be cool!

The matter of customs duty on items going into the country with you, as unaccompanied baggage, or sent in by packages during your term on the field is unpredictable. It must be taken into consideration as you plan your outfit.

Although once considered luxuries, a stove and refrigerator are generally thought of as necessities today. It may be possible for you to purchase these on the field. Or you may need to take them with you. Ask your Home Office or friends on the field.

When you decide to take appliances with you, be sure to check on the power supply and voltage in the country to which you are going. Electric razors, toasters, mixers, blenders, electric blankets, as well as stoves, refrigerators, freezers or dishwashers won't take 220 volts of power if they are made for 110. You may have to take a transformer, too.

It is a good idea to take a pretty set of plastic dishes. Certainly many an unhappy situation can be avoided by using plastic. In fact, one can even smile when a servant heads toward the kitchen with a load of dishes and that all-too-familiar clatter of a dropped tray filters back to the dining room! Certainly, however, if one has good china, sterling, crystal, and other such items on hand when preparing to leave, they should be wrapped and packed with extreme care and taken along. There is little merit in storing such items in an attic in the homeland if you intend to spend most of the rest of your life on the field. It is better that they be used on the field and perhaps damaged or destroyed than that they go untouched and unneeded at home.

For everyday use, stainless steel is adequate. It does not get "lost" or "misplaced" so readily. But today, many missionaries have the privilege of entertaining local and national officials at teas, meals and social functions. Although not trying to be ostentatious, it is always in good taste to provide the very best on such occasions by setting a beautiful table with lace cloth, fine china, crystal and sterling.

Probably of all the comforts of home, an individual's bed is the most appreciated. Rope beds, stone beds, or lumpy cotton mattresses can prove to be intolerable. For this reason, you may want to take a comfortable roll-away bed or a box spring and mattress for each family member. Again this decision must ever be based on information received from the mission, the field, and according to your own budget limits.

Don't forget a raincoat, footwear and an umbrella. Be sure to take a typewriter. Some missions require secretaries to take an office typewriter, but every missionary or missionary family should have a portable typewriter in his possession. In some cases it can be

arranged to have special characters on your machine
which will allow you to type in both English and Spanish,
German, Portuguese, French, or other languages. Take
a good camera and a supply of film. Usually a 35mm is
best, although some will want a movie camera as well.
Camping equipment and light nylon bedrolls are useful.
A car, Jeep, truck, Land Rover, trailer, or other
conveyance should be considered carefully. Seek field
advice on this matter.

When you arrive on the field, there is nothing more
pleasant than making your house a familiar home. No
matter of what material this house may be constructed -
mud, stucco, wood, brick, mortar, grass - having a few
favorite items from the homeland is essential. Perhaps
it will be a picture which has long been a part of
your life, or a piece of furniture. For the children
it could be a stuffed animal or a worn toy. It might
be a small rug at the entryway, or ruffled curtains in
the living room. But this will be your home so remember to take a few things to help produce a real home
atmosphere.

On most mission fields there are a few items which
are not readily available, but which, if taken with
you, are a great joy to you and your fellow workers as
time goes by. Along this line we would include such
things as paper napkins, birthday candles and decorations,
note paper, ball point pens, inexpensive games, birthday, get-well and anniversary cards, Christmas cards and
ornaments, coat hangars, curtain rods, tacks, pins,
towel racks, soap dishes, etc. These are not essentials,
but can be very useful.

If you play a musical instrument, take it with you.
An item as large as a piano or organ would need to be
given approval by your Board, but accordians, wind instruments, stringed instruments, and music books should
be taken along for your relaxation and the entertainment
of others. They will, of course, be of help in your
ministry, too.

A tape recorder, record player and/or a radio may
be included on your list. Many Boards require that a
tape recorder be taken for language study, and thus the
inclusion of a few musical tapes will not add appre-

ciably to the weight or worth of the equipment. If you
do not want an expensive short-wave radio, do take a
small transistor radio to listen to the daily news of
your nation. This is far easier and less time consuming than struggling through a local newspaper. It
can also be an aid in learning the language.

An equipment list would not be complete without
including some very necessary items: At least one good
reference Bible in easy-to-read print; a Bible commentary
a Bible Dictionary; Bible study books. Spiritual materia
is essential and most missionaries utilize "Daily Light
on the Daily Path" or other books for personal and
family devotions. Flannelgraph stories, backgrounds and
easel should be taken. Good fiction and biographies
for adults and children are needed. Subscriptions to
religious and secular magazines should be ordered as soon
as you can give them your field address.

Do not feel obliged to purchase every item on your
equipment list. Some items will not be necessary for
YOU. Candidates have actually gone into debt to buy
things they think their mission feels are essential. One
should keep in mind the effect that a very large and expensive equipment shipment will have on both the national
and your fellow missionaries who may have very little of
this world's goods even though they have been out many
terms. Although people in the homeland are more lenient
toward missionaries having modern conveniences than previously, not every first-term missionary should take what
he thinks he will need for a life-time of service. Most
Boards will set a weight and financial limit on the amoun
of goods that can be taken to the field by a first-term
missionary. This limit has been carefully considered for
your station and you should tenaciously and faithfully
abide by the rules.

10

Where To Obtain
And Purchase Equipment

Now that you have an idea of the items which you feel you will need to take with you to the field, let's consider where these things can be obtained.

1. You may have clothing and household goods which you will take with you from your own home.

2. Friends will give you various items, either things they have that you might be able to use, or things you need that they are willing to supply for you.

3. Churches and friends will often give a going-away shower to missionary ladies. Many useful clothing and household items are obtained in this way. (If you have been told ahead of time about such a shower, and you have opportunity to request it, do urge folks to carry this out at least six weeks in advance of your leaving for the field. A shower the day before you are leaving produces some terrible packing headaches)!

4. You will have funds set apart for outgoing equipment expenditures. You are free to purchase items which you feel you will need from these funds. (Make sure to stay within the limits established by your Board for this).

Much consideration needs to be given to the quality
and price of items to be taken or purchased. As a
matter of fact, you may not feel every item donated to
you personally or through a shower will be of enough
value to you to take it half-way around the world.

Although some will be taking a washer from the homeland, many missionaries still must rely on the dhobi or
washerman to do the laundry. This is always an interesting event since their soap usually consists of lye and
grease mixed into a soap compound; their washing board
is a rock in the middle of a small stream, canal, river,
or gutter;their dryer is the parched ground in the hot
sun. Starch comes from potato or rice water (and don't
be surprised when your underwear and pajamas are as
stiff as a board and your dresses and shirts hang limply.
These folks are not acquainted with the various parts of
western clothing)! Because of the hard wear your
clothes will be getting, it is usually penny-wise and
pound foolish to buy the cheapest quality clothing.
Neither will you spend a fortune on fancy, elegant appa-
rel. But the best quality and the best price need to
be considered. Clothes guaranteed "color-fast" will
not hold their color forever under the above-described
circumstances. But they will hold up longer than
clothing which will "run".

Your ironing may need to be done with a kerosene
or charcoal iron and the heat cannot be easily regulated.
Therefore, unless you like scorched clothes, it is good
to purchase either a fabric that can be ironed with a
fairly hot iron, or one that needs no ironing at all.
(Remember again that those who may do your ironing do
not usually have a knowledge of various types of materials
and settings on an iron).

Of course, you may be planning to do your own washing
and ironing to preserve your clothing and linens. But
on the field, in the heat, where sixteen-hour days are
common, or when you're down with an attack of malaria
or dysentery, your plans for family washing and ironing
may run amuck. So do not set your compass on plans of
this type.

In many cases, store owners will give a discount to
"religious workers". It is never out of place to ask if

a store has such a policy. But NEVER BEG FOR DISCOUNTS.
Do not expect that a businessman should lose his profit
on merchandise or services just because you happen to
be a missionary candidate.

There are organizations which are subsidized by
gifts from Christian groups and individuals so they
can offer regulation items of all kinds at greatly reduced prices. Discount houses, and wholesale outlets,
and companies specializing in overseas shipments may
offer extremely favorable prices. Some Mission Offices
have supplies of drugs and other items at greatly reduced
prices readily available for their personnel. Check
with your Home Office concerning the names and addresses
of suppliers.

Keep in mind how your equipment items will be shipped
to you. If they are to go by air, weight is a serious
factor. If you purchase on the West Coast and expect
to fly or sail from the East coast (or vice versa) you
should keep in mind that it will be far less expensive
to purchase the needed articles near the place from
which they will be shipped. In some cases this is not
possible. But, for example, those living in Minneapolis
who will be going to Latin America would do well to purchase large articles of equipment and appliances in
Miami, thus saving overland shipping costs.

Be sure to consider known government regulations
concerning the import of items into the country in which
you will be serving. Some countries will not allow the
import of articles made of wood. Others will not allow
certain food items. Still others prohibit new shoes.
You may pay 100 to 200% duty on a car or truck in some
lands and this is a definite consideration in purchasing
items of this magnitude.

In most countries of the world today, you are able to
purchase the normal commodities of life. If at all
possible, consult before purchasing articles in these lands.
It is possible that ready-made items are much more expensive and not as nicely made as those that are custom-
made to your specifications. It is also possible that
items can be obtained from others who are leaving the
country (government workers, other missionaries, etc.).

11

Financial Matters

One of the first questions an accepted candidate is going to raise is "what do I live on while I'm engaged in deputation work?"

In Faith Mission Board practice, there is no guarantee of salary from the Mission Board for living expenses from the moment of acceptance. In most cases, the candidate will continue in a full-time job and take week-end and evening meetings close to his home. Many are able to obtain their full support in this way, and thus work until the time they leave for the field. Most employers are also sympathetic in allowing time off from work for special meetings if the privilege is not misused.

Some Boards allow the candidate certain travel allowance money from his own account, from the funds received at meetings, or from the Mission's General Account. He is not allowed to use more funds than he has in one of these accounts.

If a person feels led to terminate his employment and enter full-time deputation, he may receive special personal gifts from friends to cover expenses, be given lodging and food at no expense to him, or he may choose to use money previously saved. In any case, it would seem best not to quit a job the day your acceptance letter arrives. At least plan your meeting schedule before you give up your visible means of support. This is especially

true in the case of married couples. The Lord will
supply all your needs in unusual ways, but common sense
also has to be exercised. Some Boards allow candidates
to set a target date for leaving for the field, and
3 to 6 months previously, if funds are available in
his account, support is given each month on the same
rate as Home Mission workers.

The usual financial matters which must be cared
for before the candidate can leave for the field are:

1. Missionary support (In the case of those
    planning to be married, or expecting to raise
    a family on the field, it is necessary to take
    this into account when raising support).

2. Travel funds sufficient to cover transportation,
    shipment of baggage to the field, and estimated
    customs duty.

3. Outfit and equipment. The range of needs will
    be great in this category. Some folks can get
    by with very little. Others feel they must have
    a great deal. Many missions set a limit on the
    value of outfits an individual is allowed. In
    this case, set your priorities carefully.

4. Language School expenses if the Candidate is
    to attend.

When offerings are received from a church or individual, they should be sent to the Home Office with full
details concerning the donor and address so an official
tax-deductible receipt may be sent. These funds are put
into the candidate's designated fund. If personal gifts
are received, no mission receipt needs to be sent unless
requested by the donor. The candidate, however, may
elect to put this money into his travel or outfit fund.

Your mission will probably request monthly or
quarterly financial reports from you, indicating the
name and full address of each donor, amount received,
purpose for which it was specified, whether it was sent
to the Home Office, and if not, how it was utilized.

Remember that you will need to plan on at least 1/3

to 1/2 of the declared value of your outfit and equipment to ship it to your field and pay customs on it.

Be certain your supporters understand the financial setup of your particular Board. Explain Work Support, Missionary Support, Project Support, Passage and Equipment, Personal Gifts, etc. Ask them to contact the Home Office at any time they have questions. Also ask them to check their receipts each time they send a gift. If you are listed with your mission as a number, a set of initials, or a Project, be sure to confide this to your supporters. This is the only way they can tell if their gift has actually been credited to YOUR account. A receipt which gives their support to #51 or Project X will not be meaningful if they aren't aware that you are listed that way with your mission. Then if they get a receipt marked differently, they can question the Accounting Office. (Believe it or not, no matter how careful, there have been mixups in the number, initial and project systems, even when fed into computers).

Do not hold funds received from meetings for more than a week or two. Some candidates insist on holding funds to send with their monthly or quarterly reports. This may save time and postage, but it produces hard feelings with donors who expect rapid expediting of their gifts, and rightly so.

Most missions set the support figures needed for each adult and for each child 0-5 years, 6-11 years, 12 years through High School and High School graduates through college or age 21. These amounts will be discussed with you thoroughly upon your acceptance. Some missions are now establishing a salary scale, also.

Most Boards will allow a candidate to obtain over-support of between 10 and 20% of the annual support figure. This is not a requirement, but in the event extra support is pledged, it is allowed to this extent since it is used to build up the account. If your financial needs change during your term of service, it may come in especially handy. If your Mission pools all support, this over-support can be of help to others who may have had difficulty raising needed funds. In Boards where a monthly salary is received, the extra funds will build up the individual's account to be used for travel or other bona fide expenses which normally come from the support account.

Each candidate should feel a sincere responsibility in the matter of raising support. Even in the case where a Board may allow the candidate to leave for the field without full support, every effort should be made to raise the amounts required.

If your mission sets a financial limit on the value of equipment you are allowed to take to the field, it is essential that you make a fair declaration of the items you are taking. It must also be kept in mind that included in the total amount will be those funds which you will set aside to purchase necessary equipment items on the field. For some fields, this can be a sizeable amount. Be honest in your estimation of these expenses added to those items which you will take with you or send from the homeland.

The financial aspect of our lives may be the most difficult of all to dedicate wholly to the Lord. And yet money is only a commodity loaned to us by Him for our use. It is certainly not the most important thing in our lives. It cannot buy happiness, peace, security, health. It cannot love or respect you. It is a fine servant but a despotic master. In many senses "the love of money is the root of all evil." (I Timothy 6:10).

Before entering the future, be sure to seek answers to some of these questions:

...Am I happy about the prospect of living on a sub-standard salary?

...Am I, a doctor or engineer, satisfied to receive the same monthly support as a teacher, secretary, nurse or Bible teacher?

...Will the lack of financial remuneration become a stumbling block to my ministry?

...Can I trust God concerning finances when I long for better things for my children and nicer things for my home?

...Is it in my nature to be envious if my co-workers
receive large personal gifts and I receive none?

...Suppose my co-worker insists on food items which
I feel are unnecessary, but for which I have to
pay my share?

...Who owns my purse?

At this moment you will slough off these questions.
But there will come a good many times in the days ahead
when this will be a very serious matter.

Men and women have left the mission field by the
scores over the simple matter of finances. When they
left the homeland, they completely understood the financial policies of the Mission. They knew exactly how
much they would receive, where it would come from, and
how often they would receive it. They knew of the
possibility of the support scale being raised during
their term of service. They realized folks at home
might have to drop their support for one reason or another
They knew additional children would bring additional
expenses. But in the midst of the battle, it was not easy
to struggle with financial matters. They never went to
bed hungry and they had the necessities of life, but others
seemed to have more, or they looked back and thought of
what they could have had in the way of material things
back in the homeland. And they've left the field discouraged and lacking fruit. Oh, candidate, before you
leave for your service, get this matter of finances
settled in your own heart and mind. God is not a pauper.
Where He guides, He supplies. Trust Him fully in this
matter today and in the days ahead. If you honestly
cannot do so, determine right now that you will not go
to the field.

If a candidate withdraws from his Mission prior to
his going to the field, there should be an accurate
accounting of all funds received. Unless there is a request from the donor for redesignation, all such funds
are turned over to be used in the Mission work as the
Director or Board deems fitting and proper. Personal
salary, gifts and deputation expenses are not usually reimbursed, although some candidates feel responsible to
return these funds to the mission or the donor from their
personal finances.

If friends want to give you money for a particular part of your outfit, send all such gifts to the Home Office designated for that purpose so that proper receipts may be issued.

Any bills for equipment purchases sent to the Home Office for payment need authorization from you. For regular payments on Mutual Funds, insurance premiums, etc., be sure to give clear instructions to your Home Office and a source of personal funds to pay for these.

The candidate should make arrangements to carry sufficient money with him in Travelers Checks when leaving for the field to cover baggage costs, first month's living expenses and incidentals. A full accounting of such funds should be given to the Home Office.

12

Medical And Dental Matters

Although most Boards are very careful concerning
medical and dental matters, some do not require a
thorough medical and dental examination before the
candidate is accepted for service. Other Boards do
not check through on questionable items contained in
these reports (history of nervous breakdown, allergies,
heart disease as a child, susceptibility to certain
diseases, diabetes, etc.) In other cases an examination is required during the application process but the
candidate may not actually leave for the field for a
period of two to three years, with no further examination requested. During the intervening time there may
have been a serious problem, an operation, the birth
of a child, or several other matters which have caused,
or are causing, physical concern to the candidate.

Although we find that medical and dental facilities
on the various mission fields of the world today are
much improved, there are still many areas where good
professional help is not immediately available. Some
missions operate their own clinics and hospitals and
have their own doctors and nurses; many do not. Some
governments operate efficient, well-kept facilities that
are perfectly acceptable for westerners to patronize.
But ín the out-of-the-way places, it is still possible
to have to travel 500 or 1,000 miles in order to obtain
good medical treatment. Emergencies do arise on the
mission field. But if there is a tendency toward illness
in a special realm,it is good to have this cared for at

home, or at a time when it may not take your life or
ruin the effectiveness of your ministry.

Dental care is probably less adequate in most places
than medical care. Therefore, it is imperative that all
needs be cared for at home. For those who wear artificial
dentures or bridgework, it would be wise, if possible,
to take an extra set with you. It is amazing what
stripping sugar cane can do to false teeth! (Or, for
that matter, teeth have been broken off on less dangerous
items such as a slice of toast or a piece of camel meat).

It is also important to have a good eye examination
before you leave the homeland. Glasses are not obtain-
able for your prescription except in the larger cities.
(Be sure to carry a prescription for your lenses). Carry
at least one extra pair of glasses. For all practical
purposes, contact lenses are less available to you and
may prove troublesome in extremely hot, dusty or other
unfavorable climates. You would do well to have at
least one pair of prescription sunglasses as well. It
is true with many people that they have had perfectly
normal vision when leaving for the field only to find that
constant language study, reading up and down or from right
to left rather than in the normal left to right pattern,
has taken its toll and once strong eyesight begins to
weaken. If trouble occurs, be sure to have it checked
the first opportunity you have to be near an eye doctor
on the field, but be sure he is reputable, for poorly-
fitted or wrongly-prescribed glasses can cause as much
or more trouble than no glasses at all.

If you should find yourself in a mission which does
not require a thorough medical or dental examination
each year, for your own sake, be sure to get a check-up
before you leave the homeland, including chest X-rays.
If any medication is required, take a sufficient quantity
with you. If treatment is recommended, have this cared
for. Sick missionaries are not an asset to the work,
and although the unexpected illnesses will come to one
and all in the course of events, some of the major problems can be cared for by a simple but thorough examination before departure.

During the last two months before leaving for the
field, it is essential to obtain all shots and vaccina-

tions required for the area where you will be serving.
A smallpox vaccination is necessary. Be sure you know
when booster shots are needed and obtain them. Many
folks get no reaction to any of their shots. Others
will have some discomfort from them. Unless there is
a real allergy to the vaccine, a couple of aspirin (if
you are not allergic to them) and good use of the
affected arm will help reduce the pain and fever which
sometimes accompanies typhoid, para-typhoid, tetanus,
yellow fever, and other shots. Be sure to set up a
schedule to receive your shots so they will be completed
at least two weeks before your anticipated departure
date. Check with the Home Office of your Mission concerning the immunizations required for your field of
service. These will vary. You will need to find the
best possible sources of vaccine for each shot required.
Yellow fever is usually given only by a Government
Office or an agency authorized by them. You may wish
to receive your other shots from your family doctor.
In some areas, free immunizations may be obtained from
the local Public Health Department. Check with them on
this possibility and be sure to find out what days the
various immunizations are given. If, on the other
hand, you are acquainted with a nurse, she may be able
to work with a doctor on this. She would administer
the shots and the doctor would sign the certificate.
This could save the family money. In all events, be
sure your health card is duly signed, authorized and
notarized with appropriate notations by the covering
doctor, Public Health Officer and other legal stamps,
seals and signatures.

Be sure you know if your Mission Board has a medical
plan. Understand what benefits you receive from such a
plan and what responsibilities fall to you if you require
medical or hospital treatment. As one who may not yet be
considered an "employee" or "salaried member" of your
mission, be sure to have medical coverage of your own
until your insurance becomes effective with your Board.
There is often a time limit stipulation as to when an
"appointee" may be included in the overall program of the
mission.

A word should be mentioned concerning medical matters
pertaining to members of your family who will remain in
the homeland. Often a missionary will leave for the

field knowing a mother and/or father is ill and in need
of medical attention. This is a matter which must be
entrusted to the Lord, and plans must be made for the
care of those for whom you are responsible. In some
cases it may mean making arrangements to admit the sick
relative to a Rest Home or Nursing Center. For others
it may mean having someone stay in the home during your
absence. It might even require you to delay your going
to the field for several months or indefinitely. Such
situations are very difficult, but they must be settled
before you leave. In a day when missionaries can fly
around the world very quickly, it is a temptation to
leave a medical matter hanging in mid-air, assuming that
if the situation worsens, a flight home can readily and
easily be arranged. But we must give some thought to
what happens in Language School or on the field when a
person is suddenly removed from the scene. We need also
to consider the extra expense involved in this additional
travel. Of course, emergencies do arise, but if there
is a situation which can be handled before you leave,
be sure to take care of it now.

13

Legal Matters

Missionaries do not go to the field with the feeling that they will give their lives for the cause of Christ, although they are willing to do so, if necessary. With this in mind, there are several legal matters which should be taken into consideration before the candidate leaves the homeland.

One of the most important documents in anyone's life is a WILL. Even though you may feel you have nothing of importance to leave to posterity, it is still important that you have a will properly executed and filed. In the case of missionary parents, it is essential that your will contain an indication as to who the guardian of your children will be in the event that you should both be killed or die of natural causes. The exact designation of property, personal belongings, bank account jewelry, etc., should be indicated. An executor must be named for your estate.

INSURANCE may be carried on your life by the mission, or by yourself. Be sure that this clearly indicates who your beneficiary will be in the event of your death.

Your POWER OF ATTORNEY should be given to a close friend, relative, or lawyer in the homeland in the event legal papers need to be signed during your absence on the field. This is a very highly important power and therefore should be entrusted only to one well-known and respected by you.

For those of draft age, it is important that you keep your DRAFT BOARD notified at all times of your present address and occupation. If there is a change in your occupation, this should be noted. When forms are sent, they should be filled out and returned at once to the draft board. In the case of missionary candidates, it is usual for the mission board to write to the draft board upon the acceptance of the candidate for service, and to keep the board informed concerning his occupation and whereabouts if requested by the Draft Board to do so.

A PASSPORT must be obtained if you are leaving the country. The occupation listed should be your profession or status. If you are going strictly for evangelical preaching, it might be listed as "missionary". For many, however, this occupation will rightly be stated as secretary, administrator, printer, engineer, doctor, nurse, housewife, pilot, teacher, musician, etc. Check with your mission concerning their preference for you in this matter. Take special note of the renewal date for your passport. Do not let it lapse. Decide if you want your entire family included on one passport or individual passports for each member. (Keep in mind that if there is but one passport and more than one member is required to travel at the same time to different countries, it will be impossible. And if one member has the passport for a trip outside the country, the others are left without official papers. This must be weighed against the cost of additional passports).

Various countries require VISAES and ENTRANCE PAPERS. In some cases someone on the field must obtain RESIDENCE PAPERS for you before your arrival. Be sure to be aware of the government regulations concerning the country to which you are going as well as the requirements of your own government in this matter. Your home office will probably handle these matters for you. In some cases, if you attend Language School in a country other than the one to which you have been assigned, entrance papers for your field of service cannot be obtained from the homeland. In such an event, the Field Director will handle the details for you. Be sure to give him complete information by the quickest possible means when it is requested from you. If you are the first from your mission to enter a new field, some of this work may be done by an older,

well-established board already at work there. Such
rapport and helpfulness between missions is usually the
rule on the field.

It would be well to check with your local SOCIAL
SECURITY office concerning various aspects of the Social
Security program so that you might better understand
your relationship to it. Your Home Office will also be
able to give you information concerning this matter.

Although you may not have to pay INCOME TAX during
your term of service because of your residence outside
of the homeland, it is possible that you have other
income (rent, stocks and bonds, bank accounts, trust
funds, interest, and the like) which would make it
necessary for you to pay each year. At any rate, an
income tax statement needs to be filed annually. Be
sure to check with your Mission Accounting Office concerning this vital matter. If there are further questions, contact your nearest office of the Internal
Revenue Service.

It might be adviseable to use the facilities of a
SAFE DEPOSIT BOX to store important legal documents
in the homeland. Some missions have facilities for
storage of important papers in their office safe.

Be sure to keep LICENSES renewed. (Nurse's Registration, Doctor's Registration, Engineer's License,
Electrician's License, Driver's License, etc.). It
may be difficult and/or time-consuming to renew these if
they have been allowed to lapse.

Many countries require you to take with you an
AFFIDAVIT FROM YOUR LOCAL POLICE DEPARTMENT showing that
you have no police record. Check with your Home Office
concerning the need for this paper.

Your HEALTH CARD showing innoculations and immunizations received should be kept with your passport at all
times. It should be kept up-to-date and duly signed and
sealed.

You may want to keep an open BANK ACCOUNT in the homeland. Deposit and withdrawal slips should be left with

the Home Office in the event you want them to transact
business for you.   In this case, the signature of a
mission officer should appear on your account.   This
is often essential when candidates attend Language
School in a country to which funds cannot be transmitted.
The Mission will deposit funds in this account and the
missionary will draw against this to receive his monthly
allotment and to pay his Language School expenses.   A
friend or relative might be able to co-sign your account
if you would prefer it.

Although your passport should serve the same purpose,
it is safe to carry a copy of the BIRTH CERTIFICATE for
each member of your family.

A copy of your ORDINATION PAPERS and DEDICATION and/or
COMMISSIONING SERVICE is required in some countries.

Always check with your Home Office to determine the
various legal matters which must be cared for before you
leave the homeland.

14

Ordination, Dedication
And/Or Commissioning Service

Many male candidates with the proper educational background and credentials will want to become an ordained Christian minister before going to the field. This is most appropriate, even though your main ministry may not be as a pastor of a church. On out-of-the-way stations and in situations where there are few missionaries involved in the work, it is most appropriate for the missionary to be an ordained man with the legal right of marrying and burying Christians, and performing other pastoral functions. (Being ordained does not mean that you must use the title "pastor" or "missionary" on your passport). When you arrive on the field, be sure to find out what specific government restrictions apply to your pastoral ministry.

Dedication and/or commissioning services are usually sponsored by your home church or Bible School. On many fields today, it is essential that such a service be held, and a copy of the certificate received at that service must be turned over to the proper authorities on the field to establish the fact that you are, indeed, in that land for specific Christian work. Younger men may need this certificate to send to their draft board. Women may also need this to qualify for certain benefits.

The pastor of your home church, supporting church, or the leaders of the Bible School you attended will usually perform this service. It is your prerogative to have an official from your mission present and to take part in it.

If furlough folks from your mission are in the area, or other candidates, invite them and perhaps allow them to take part in the service. This is a time of publicly being set apart for service on the field. It can be very meaningful to the candidate and challenging to those who attend - more so, perhaps, if you are going out from your home church.

If you are responsible for the plans for this service, be sure to prepare well in advance and send word to your mission office concerning it. Some Home Offices have commissioning certificates available for your use, or they can be obtained from a Bible Book Store.

In some cases, a commissioning service cannot be held until your preparation for the field is complete and the Board of Directors votes for your commission of appointment as a missionary. Other Boards view all candidates as having been commissioned and appointed before the official service takes place.

The service may be brief and informal, or may take the place of a regularly scheduled meeting, or may be a special meeting called for this purpose. Missionary hymns are sung. The candidate is allowed an opportunity to give his testimony. There should then be a challenge for prayer support with a time of dedication and prayer following led by the pastor of your home church, a representative from your Board, the Chairman of the Missionary Committee of the host church, and/or specially invited guests. This is a time of serious commitment on the part of the candidate as well as for those in the church to uphold the missionary with prayer and financial support.

Programs may be printed outlining the service, or if it is a part of a longer service, a special announcement in the bulletin will suffice. Often there is a reception at the church or in the home of one of the members following the service so that friends can greet the candidate informally and assure him of support during the days and years to follow.

15

Your Relationship
To Your Mission Board

From the time your application is submitted to the Board you have chosen, you are committed to them and responsible to supply any and all information they request, inasmuch as possible to speak at services arranged by them for you, to notify them of your itinerary and where you can be reached at all times.

A copy of each prayer letter should be sent to both the Home Office and the Central Field Headquarters (if the two are in different locations).

Prayer cards should be on file with the mission.

Funds received in meetings should be sent in regularly with reports.

The Board should be kept well informed as to how much support you have, what is lacking, your goal date for reaching the field (or Language School).

Nearer the time of your departure, an equipment list should be sent for approval.

If your Board has to prepare papers or provide for the shipment of equipment, they must know the details, values, insurance requested, date to expect the shipment and other such details.

Whenever your Board asks questions, answer them.   They

would not request information without a good reason for
needing it. Even when you can't see why certain details
are being requested from you, TRUST YOUR BOARD, and
supply the answers they need.

If you ever have questions concerning policies or
procedures, contact your Board at once.

In all of your meetings, defend your Board with 100%
of your being. If you lack confidence in your Board,
either change your attitude or choose another Board.
Even though there is room for improvement in all human
institutions, it is neither logical nor meaningful to
destroy confidence in your organization. There is no
sense in thinking you are going to change the entire
trend of a Board which has been functioning and doing a
commendable job for the past 30, 50 or 100 years. Nor
will you gain any merit for yourself or the work of the
Lord by sharing inner-mission problems with "outsiders".
Remember, too, as a candidate you are not able to view
the total picture accurately. Therefore, withhold your
judgment of anything or anyone until you are able to
provide an answer that will solve the matter in question.
It doesn't take brilliance to criticize and condemn. It
may take a great degree of patience and spiritual strength
to wait for the answers to be worked out in a manner
which is Biblically sound and personally acceptable.
Again, trust your Board and its leadership.

Be thoroughly conversant with the Constitution, By-
Laws, and Principles and Practices of your Board. Make
yourself familiar with all provisions and demands of
the Board.

When you are transacting business with the Home Office,
be sure to include a separate note concerning each item
you want handled. For example, monthly reports may not
go to the same individual as requests for items to be
purchased. Do not send a general letter to the Director
which includes items of business for several individuals.

If you, as a single person, become engaged to be
married, notify your Board immediately. Unless your
fiancee is also a candidate or a missionary under your
Board, your engagement will change your status with

respect to your candidacy. If children are added to your family, give your Mission full details.

You must maintain effective communications with your Board at all times. They are your closest friend and ally as pertains to questions needing answers, policies needing clarification and work which needs to be accomplished. Get to know your Home Office staff and Mission leaders.

You ARE your mission to all who come in contact with you. What you are now determines what your Board is. And you will also determine in the minds of Christian friends what the future of your Board will be. You are a member of a team and must function as such. Decisions made without official approval can affect the entire structure and outreach of your Board. Work in conjunction with the other members of your team. You cannot do the job by youself, and neither can they.

16

What You May Expect
From Your Home Office

Your Home Office is a vital segment of your missionary experience. Its dedicated Christian workers are your friends. They desire God's highest and best for you and are willing to help you in every way to attain to it. They want to know your prayer burdens. They follow your deputation ministry with interest. They eagerly await the day when you are on your way to the field.

If you have any questions concerning finances, mission policies, requirements, equipment, or any other of a thousand things, they stand ready to give a prompt response in person, by letter, or by telephone.

If you need stationery, literature or other supplies, it is available through the office. When you need report forms, they'll be happy to send them.

You should expect to receive periodic statements concerning your financial standing, and the various donors who have sent in funds.

The Home Office should be able to supply you with a definite equipment list, a complete and personal financial sheet showing your actual requirements for the field. They should notify you when it is time to apply for your passport. They should either apply for, or give you information concerning applying for your visa and/or entrance papers and work permits. They should give you a list of required immunizations and when they should be received.

If your mission has area representatives, be sure to check with your Director to understand what business, if any, should be handled through this representative.

You should receive news items from your field through the Home Office. You should be on their mailing list to receive regular mailings unless your Board sends packets of these materials to each candidate.

You may be able to obtain a film, curios, slide-tape series and/or display from the office. They may also be able to give you requests for speakers they have received from your area. (Do not, however, expect the home office to obtain your support for you if you are expected to secure it for yourself. Do not expect the office to do your work for you. It is there to help you do your work more effectively and efficiently).

Check to see if your important papers can be left in the mission safe, or what alternate plan they may have available for this purpose.

If you have questions to ask of missionaries on the field and do not know any of them personally, the Home Office may send your questions by ham radio contact or in official correspondence. Or they may give you the name(s) of individuals who could best answer your request.

You will be amazed at the many details the Home Office cares for on your behalf. The longer you serve with the Mission, the more you will appreciate the many services available to you - from receipting your support funds, to purchasing equipment at discount; from answering questions, to transporting you to the ship or the airport when the day of departure arrives. Be grateful for these faithful workers and avail yourself freely of the services they offer you.

Most office staffs spend definite segments of time each week in united prayer on your behalf. And there have been occasions when an office person has felt led of the Lord to take on some support for a candidate.

Because your Home Office is set up to serve you in so many different ways, it is sometimes the case that some will try to take advantage of this. Unless some-one specifically volunteers to do it, do not expect that one of the staff members will house you and your family for a week or two before you leave for the field, or that someone will be kind enough to purchase various personal supplies. Unless your Board is an exceedingly small one, the office staff just cannot do the things which you, with a little forethought and planning, can do for yourself.

17

Your Relationship To
Your Supporters

It hardly seems necessary to remind you that it is imperative for you to keep in contact with those who are supporting you by their gifts and prayers. As soon as the Mission notifies you of gifts sent to your account, write a note of thanks to each donor. Even a postcard will do. A friendly word, genuine gratitude and the certain knowledge that you appreciate their gift (in some cases, a sacrifice) will establish true Christian fellowship and friendship with those who will make it possible for you to serve. In a real sense you are co-laborers together with Christ. Your supporters are not under obligation to continue your support indefinitely, but the more you can do to show your sincere appreciation for their ministry, the more interested they will be in caring for your needs.

Under no circumstances should you feel it is the duty of your friends to send funds to your account because you are in full-time Christian service. Remember that they work for THEIR money, too. And what do any of us have which we have not received from Him? Your friends support you because they have confidence in your ability not to let them down. They feel they are making a wise investment of their money. But you must cause them to continue to feel you are worthy of this interest. A laborer is worthy of his hire. Are you giving a full measure of work as a candidate? And do you give your supporters an indication of what you are accomplishing so that their funds will produce eternal dividends? Are you sending them prayer requests and answers to prayer? Are you thoughtfully keeping in touch? If not, you will suffer loss, for support will drop; and your mission will lose out because friends will judge it by you. A newsletter will never take the place of a personal note from you.

Be sure to pray for your supporters, too. And if, as often happens, a child or teen-ager pledges toward your support, be especially careful to write to him. Although these gifts may be small in comparison to those received from adults, it can change a young person's entire attitude toward Christianity in general, and missions in particular, if you will take the time to correspond with him. Always send your letters directly to the child and not to his parents. Make them personal and informative. You have the opportunity of paving the pathway for a future missionary.

Never hint to your supporters that you have special financial needs in the hope that they will feel sorry for you and send you extra gifts. Some may ask you from time to time if you need anything. In this case, be prepared to give an honest answer.

If your children receive personal gifts from individuals, or specified support gifts, and they are old enough to write, be sure they send a note of thanks. Don't do it for them. Contributors appreciate the uninhibited expression of gratitude they receive from children.

Never put your security in your supporters or their money. Your confidence must always and ever be in the God Who is enough. HE supplies your needs - through people, yes - but through people who give their money to the Lord, even though it may be designated for you. And thus it is a loan to you from Him. You are serving Him and not your supporters. This, of course, makes your responsibility great. Your supporters usually realize this, and thus they will pray for you and have a special interest in your ministry along with giving their financial gifts. Don't disappoint them by ignoring them. They are, after all, your line of supply. Without them you could not serve. Contact with your supporters and gratefulness for them are priority matters. Be sure to treat them as such.

As happens so many times within the family circle, it seems that it is easy to neglect those who are the nearest and best-known to us. If relatives, or close friends pled to your support, be sure to thank them just as sincerely and appreciatively as you do those who are strangers to you. Even though you may write more often and openly to these folks, it is easy to forget to say "thank you".

18

Preparation And Shipment
Of Outfit And Equipment

Although there are a number of companies that special-
ize in crating and shipping, unless you are thoroughly
familiar with the organization, it is usually better to
pack your own baggage as much as possible. If baggage
is to be sent by ship, steel drums can be utilized and
are good for storage purposes on the field. Before
shipping, make certain they are packed solidly, are spot
welded on top to inhibit pilfering and are securely pad-
locked. In this day of air travel, however, there will
be less need for the steel drum. Fibre drums are now
utilized since they are both lightweight and sturdy. They
can be secured properly, and they, too, make fine storage
areas on the field.

Much of your baggage can be packed in foot lockers
or sturdy cartons and banded with steel. If items are
being sent via air freight, cumbersome wooden crates are
not necessary. Some countries even have laws regarding
the import of wood. You will, of course, have hand
baggage and odd items (guitar or other musical instrument,
tennis racket, baby carriage, tape recorder, etc.) which
will be handcarried.

In every case, be sure your baggage is clearly and
distinctly identified. With barrels, it is wise to stencil
your full name and port of debarkation on both the top
and side of each piece. Foot lockers should also contain
this information on top and bottom. Other luggage should

contain your full name and address inside each case as
well as on a tag on the handle. All these items will
have the company shipping tag on them, but these do not
include your name. Be sure to number each piece, and
as you pack, make a list of items in each box or package,
making sure the number on your list corresponds to the
appropriately numbered container. It is a good idea
to have at least six copies of this list with you. You
must have it when going through customs. One list should
give the approximate RESALE value of each item. Another
list should give the REPLACEMENT value of each item for
insurance purposes.

Clothing and shoes should be worn at least once, and
linens laundered before packing. This, then, will be
listed as USED clothing.

Appliances should be used before packing so (1) they
can be declared used and (2) you will know they are in
working condition before taking them with you.

Always check with the Field Director or a missionary
friend on the field before taking large items of equipment. Special permit papers may be required. Or certain
items may be prohibited.

In some cases, your Board will handle the arrangements
for shipping. In others, the Mission's official shipping
agent will handle these matters, and in yet others, the
missionary is responsible to locate his own agent, airline
or freight company. This should be done with care and
upon the advice of an experienced person. If crates are
needed, it is usually less expensive to make them yourself
than to have them made. If large items are purchased, the
can usually be ordered packed for overseas delivery. Some
stores have special offices that handle only overseas
shipments.

If you have permission to send your baggage ahead to
your Home Office, or another location at the port of debarkation, be sure to put your name and the mission address
indicating clearly that this is to be trans-shipped to
your field address.

If items are sent to an air freight or other company,

be sure they do not arrive more than 30 days before they are to be shipped. Storage charges turn into money. As soon as items are shipped to your forwarder, send a letter to the company specifying in detail the number of pieces, kinds, when and how they were sent, and a copy of the waybill, if possible. Ask them to expect these and request that they be held for shipment on a certain date and give complete shipping instructions. Also indicate whether more pieces will be added to the shipment from companies, and if so, which ones. Also identify further pieces you may bring to them personally at the time of your departure. Usually if the same agents are used by a Board for all new and returning missionaries, the company is most helpful and careful in handling your outfit.

Some foreign countries require a person to have arrived in the country before any baggage can be received in his name. In such a situation, it is important to make sure your things are sent AFTER you have left the homeland. Usually this is set for from one to three days following your departure, depending on the loads the line will be handling during that period and the number of flights they make to that country.

For those who will spend from six months to a year in Language School, other problems arise. Since it is not wise, and in many cases it is illegal, to ship goods into a country before your arrival, you have to plan on sending only what is absolutely necessary to your Language School address if it is not in the same field as your country of work (which is true with many missionaries to Latin America who study language in Costa Rica, Mexico or Bolivia). A friend in the homeland would then have to be appointed to keep your goods for you, sending them at the time you indicate, making sure they contact the agent at the point of departure from the homeland. In some cases where a mission has storage room or a warehouse, they can handle receipt of baggage at the time you leave for Language School and then ship it when you arrive on the field. Or you may find it necessary to put your things in storage with a warehouse at the point of future shipment. This is the most awkward course of action, and most expensive, but sometimes necessary.

When making your list of items for customs purposes,
it is not necessary to list each pair of socks and each
piece of underwear, or each pot and pan. Generalize
your categories, i.e., personal effects, household items,
books, clothing, etc. You should be specific on items
such as a typewriter, tape recorder, radio or other small
appliances. Also be sure to keep a record of the serial
numbers of all such goods including cameras.

Be sure to check on insurance coverage for your
baggage. You may want to take out extra insurance to
cover your shipment both within the homeland and overseas

Check with your Mission Board concerning the agent
who will be handling your baggage on the receiving end.
It may be a company, or it may be an agent appointed by
your mission for this express purpose. Many times a
national affiliated with your mission is appointed to
this position and does an excellent job.

When you, personally, depart the country, be sure to
state to the airline or shipping agent how many pieces
of unaccompanied luggage you are having sent. Keep the
original bill of lading with your important documents.
You will need it when going through customs. Also inform
the customs officials the exact number of items being sent
to you as unaccompanied baggage.

New missionaries are often asked by missionaries on
the field or by the mission itself to take items for
other people on the field. Customs usually looks down
upon this practice. If, however, you care to be troubled
with such items, make sure you have given permission in
writing, and then keep a record of whose articles you
are taking, weight involved and customs duty paid to be
reimbursed by the missionary involved if you care to do
so. If your shipment has been completed and you do not
wish to add other items to yours, it is in order to write
a letter of apology to the missionary stating you find it
impossible to carry out his request. Items should never
become part of your outgoing equipment unless o.k.'d by
you beforehand.

After you have notified the proper authorities concerning the exact number of unaccompanied items you have

sent, do not expect to be able to have other items
added as an afterthought. Unless initially listed upon
your entry, equipment comes to you through the usual
channels, and may have a high duty rate attached. In
some countries such parcels would be financially pro-
hibitive. In others, they would be disallowed.

When packing, be sure to utilize your space to the
best possible advantage. Stuff shoes with small, soft
items. Pack breakables in soft towels or linens. Put
appliances in the midst of clothing. If packed correctly,
your baggage should need very little or no extra padding.
It is wise to note that you should not pack soap in the
same container with dry foodstuffs, or moth balls with
candy (unless extensively and securely wrapped in
aluminum foil). You should guard against putting any
items together which will be ruined by the association.
Plastic bags can be utilized to great advantage and will
come in extremely handy on the field.   Remember that
newsprint rubs off on everything it touches!

If you have ever watched freight being loaded or
unloaded, you will die a thousand deaths when you think
of what can happen to your baggage. But if it is packed
well, banded securely, locked insofar as possible and
prayed over concernedly, you will usually make out better
than you anticipated.

You may also be wondering how you get your shipment
from your home to the port of embarkation. There are
many ways of transporting this. It can be sent by Railway
Express, by truck, by car, by bus, by plane, or with
friends. Many times moving vans will be happy for your
small additional weight to complete a shipment they are
making. Be sure to discover the approximate arrival date
at the destination, and also find out what provision, if
any, is made for transporting it to your shipping agent.
Those missions which are located in the area of embarkation
may be willing to pick up and transfer your shipment. In
other cases, you will have to make other arrangements.

An additional note to short-term workers needs to be
included here. If you are to be in the foreign country for
only a few weeks or months, it is very possible you will
not be allowed to take excess baggage. You will probably
not be obtaining residence papers and without a change of

residence, only personal baggage can be taken with you.
Be prepared for heavy duty charges on excess luggage.

When shipping to some countries, the bags and boxes
should be marked to include the names of all in the
family since exemption allowance in customs is granted
on an individual basis. If they are sent in the name
of only one person, all goods above the allowable amount
for that individual may be dutiable.

One last reminder. Your outfit and equipment has
been obtained through the gifts of others or from personal
funds. You have spent a great deal of time getting just
the things you felt you wanted and needed. You are
looking forward to setting up housekeeping with the
things you are sending to the field. For some married
couples, it is the first time you have had brand new
things to put in your home. For single folks, it may be
your first attempt at setting up your own home situation.
Thus it is natural to prize highly your outfit and equipment. Keep in mind, however, that material things can
be quickly taken from you. Barrels can be lost in
transit. China can be broken. Items may be stolen.
Customs may hold up delivery of your goods for several
weeks or months and then you may find that the children
have already outgrown some of the new clothes you had
purchased for them. Occasionally an airline or shipping
strike will delay your possessions for several weeks.
Remember always to keep your values in the proper perspective. Always "set your affection on things above, not
on things on the earth." [1] Material goods are another
of God's gifts to you on loan. And if they should be
taken from you by one means or another, don't let it
ruin your whole ministry. How you take the spoiling of
your goods will certainly set the climate for how you will
react in other stress situations. Can you commit this to
the Lord in quietness and confidence? Do consider your
relationship to material possessions very carefully and
don't be bound by them. It is amazing to see how simplifi
your life will become when it is not encumbered with the
care and concern for "things". In truth, one can get by
with very little, and do so happily.

[1]   Colossians 3:2

19

Home Missionaries And
Workers In Missions Offices

Human beings form two categories. They are either
ministering or being ministered unto. They are either
saved or lost. It is a common fallacy among Christians
to think of a missionary more highly than they ought
to think. It is also a tendency to make heroes of
"foreign" missionaries merely because they have gone to
a lonely ministry "out there", wherever that might be.
And the farther away a missionary goes, the more "pity"
he receives, and perhaps more prayer support. (Nothing
is ever ALL bad)!

But what about you Home Missionaries and those
faithful few serving in Mission Offices across the
homeland? Is your ministry of less importance than that
of those serving on the borders of Nepal, amidst throng-
ing crowds in Hong Kong, or amongst hardened hearts in
Europe? NO, NO. A thousand times NO!

You may have all the conveniences of home, fresh
bread on the table, English-speaking people surrounding
you, clothes that are in style, even a barber or a hair-
dresser on the corner to help with the beautification
procedure. But you are true soldiers of the cross of
Jesus Christ. You have sought God's will and found it.
You are His love slaves. And whatever else it may entail,
you are ready to do it.

Perhaps yours is the harder missionary life. The

temptations which face you are certainly as strong as
those Satan presents to God's workers in a secluded and
demon-worshipping area in the heart of Africa. Testimony
is sustained only by dwelling in Christ and by the
prayers of those who undertake to participate in this
specialized ministry.

It takes no less devotion and dedication to work for
Him at home than it does to trust Him on foreign soil. A
Home Missionary should never minimize his ministry as he
speaks in meetings. He should never apologize for God's
choice of his place of service. He should not feel
inferior to other missionaries. He should never forget,
though, that there IS a world in need, and converts
should be thoroughly taught to support ALL His true
servants.

For those of you who are headed for the foreign field,
consider carefully these of His men and women who are
serving at home. You may envy them for not having to
leave loved ones and face the struggles of adjustments in
a foreign land. Yet while you may dwell securely in a
mission compound in a fairly large and lovely capital of
the world with few discomforts and lacks, that one whom
you envied, or looked down upon, may be struggling with
the Navajo language, or may be working in a dangerous slum
area where his life means nothing to those who kill for
the sheer pleasure of it. Or he may be preaching his heart
out, telling the Good News of Christ to dispassionate men
and women who seek the Messiah but will not accept Him.
He will be lonely, weary, discouraged. Then, too, he will
be encouraged, joyful and heartened, even as you in your
ministry.

For you who work as full-time missionaries in the
homeland, you have not chosen an easy road. At the end of
life's journey, you may have fewer souls for your hire than
the one who has found fruit among the tribal Indians in
Brazil, or amongst the elite in Paris, not because you have
not been faithful in your labors, but because God gave you
a more difficult task to do. It is good to remember that
no souls are converted apart from the ministry of the Holy
Spirit and His convicting power. Being faithful in
living and preaching the Gospel is the greatest calling
of all, wherever you are and whatever you're doing.

If it were not for Home Office Workers, the work on every field of the world would come to a startling halt. The ropes must be held on the home end, and those who respond to God's call for this ministry work hand in hand with those out on the front battle lines. The work of receipting funds, making purchases, providing travel and hospitality arrangements for those passing through, writing to churches, arranging meetings, keeping missionaries on furlough informed of field events and vice versa, providing ideas, missionaries, literature, slides, tapes and programs for missionary conferences across the country, answering questions, using a typewriter, speaking a friendly word on the phone, giving a tract to a delivery man, and a thousand other details are part of the work of you as a Home Office worker, along with prayer support for the entire missionary family. This is a very important part of the total program of world-wide missions. Ask any missionary how much he values the Home Office workers. You'll be amazed! Even though you, personally, do not hear the praise sent up on your behalf, know that it is there and be heartened in your work.

So then, those of you who have been called to work in the homeland, and in Mission Offices across the land, be encouraged. Although your work may seem obscure to some who are seeking gory tales and breathtaking experiences, your ministry is not hidden from Him who has placed His hand upon you for this very work. You are a vital link in the total chain of missionary service. Thank Him for your mission field and go forward in faith and strength.

20

Short Term And Summer Workers

In today's world of instant breakfasts, instant
success, short hops around the world by plane and fast,
accurate journeys to the moon and back, it is not sur-
prising that we are faced with situations which demand
quick action, temporary employment, and specialized
services. The United States Government has seen the
need for this type of individual and has been able to
challenge thousands of young people (and older folks,
too) with the work of the Peace Corps, VISTA, and similar
programs, providing low pay and hard work for a period of
one to two years.

Missions also began to think in terms of meeting
urgent needs by utilizing men and women in their
specialized fields on mission stations which lacked personnel, perhaps because there were too few missionaries
to fill the posts, or furloughs took essential workers
away from their stations, or there were no trained persons
in a particular position. Short term missionaries, in
most fields, have provided a very necessary service and
met crises with courage on many mission stations. Some
have even given their lives while serving.

Often a short termer is a young person who is not yet
ready to commit his entire life to missionary work, but
who is anxious to see just what missionary life is all
about, and therefore applies for from six months to two
years of service. Middle-aged people are also applying
for this type of ministry. They give, as it were, a tithe
from the middle of their lifetime to help in a specific

project. Retired folks are also becoming involved in
this endeavor, many going at their own expense to help
build buildings, work in the bookkeeping office, tune
pianos, counsel missionaries, become houseparents in
missionary schools, care for the hospitality in a large
city mission headquarters, provide medical services,
etc.

Some short termers are supported in full by their
home church. Others raise support from interested
friends and churches as full-time workers do. Some go at
their own expense. Some boards may help in support through
General Funds. Some Bible Colleges send workers with
money raised through gifts from fellow-students. Some
go under denominational auspices.

Many missions are also willing to accept a limited
number of young people (usually those of college-age) for
a period of six weeks to three months if they can fill a
need on the field. Language may be a barrier on some
fields, but there are many jobs for a summer worker even
without the language, i.e., musicians, lab technicians,
secretaries, engineers, nurses, construction workers, and
any and all who have the gift of helps and want to use
this gift to give a hand to missions.

There are disadvantages for short-term workers. They
usually do not have a broad background of the people to
whom they are going. Most do not speak the language or
dialect of the people. Many of the young workers have had
no real experience yet in their field of specialized
service. Most have not had to attend Orientation sessions
in the homeland and thus may be very uninformed or mis-
informed concerning health matters, mission policies and
practices, social amenities as they concern nationals, nor
are they acquainted with their exact responsibilities on
the field.

To the Mission Board there can be certain advantages,
however, although one would wish that ALL workers were
full-time. Often it takes a full-time worker a year to
be processed for service, another year to obtain support
and outgoing expenses, and possibly another year in
Language School. Short-term workers are processed in a
much shorter period and usually take no language study.
They are young, eager to learn, and ready to fill a vital
role.

Full-time workers are required to have formal Bible training as a pre-requisite for service.

Short-termers must have an acceptable Christian testimony, but formal training may not be required.

Full-time personnel are often delayed because support is not forthcoming.

Many short-termers provide their own support and are ready to go to the field immediately upon acceptance.

Full-timers have tons of equipment with them!

Short-termers usually live with folks already established on the field, and this, of course, eliminates the need for taking any and all household items so that the short-termer often arrives with a foot locker and a suitcase, can settle in the first day, get acquainted the next, and then plunge into the ministry for which he has offered himself.

It takes time to obtain residence papers for full-time workers.

Depending on the length of anticipated service, short-termers can often travel on a tourist visa or temporary papers with a minimum of red tape involved.

Summer workers usually are not allowed to take more than a visitor's amount of luggage into the country. Be sure to check with your Board concerning items which you CANNOT take with you.

Short-termers and summer workers are filling large gaps in the missionary ranks today. And many are later applying to the Board for full-time missionary service. At that time they must normally follow the required pattern established for all missionary candidates.

21

The Single Candidate

Sometimes the attitude toward single missionaries, both on the part of people in the churches at home, and of married couples on the field, is that because you couldn't find a mate in the homeland, you are now going to try the mission field. This, however, is true in very few instances. Most single workers have turned down proposals of marriage or have not asked for a hand in marriage in order to give full devotion and attention to the service of Christ. And although we hear more often of single women serving the Lord, we must remember that there are also many single men doing an effective work in very difficult places.

If single workers could share the most difficult part of their work, they would probably agree that it is loneliness. Married folks have each other and their families. Single folks have their work and a busy life among multitudes of people, but they can face loneliness at the end of a busy day and be far away from any with whom they can share their joys and burdens.

During your days of deputation you are free to go and come as you please. You are free from your parents, and you can put your full strength into your deputation work. You have only one mouth to feed, and although you may have to exercise faith for the next meal, there is not the responsibility of feeding your spouse and children. You can go to the field with far less equipment and you need to raise less support than a couple or a family. This means you will probably be able to leave for the field

sooner than your married fellow-workers. You should not
listen to those who feel sorry for you. You are entering a full and satisfying life.

Once you are sure of the Lord's call and after you
have been accepted by your Mission Board, you must be
careful that your calling is not changed by falling in
love with one who does not share your missionary vision.
It is a temptation. It has ruined many a missionary
career and has often ended in a second-rate marriage because of the guilt which can develop from not continuing
in the Lord's best will.

Many times the Lord honors a stand to follow Him to
the ends of the earth by allowing a life partner to
enter your life at Candidate School, Orientation, Language
School, or on the field. But there are far worse things
that could happen to you than being single. It is true
that as a single person, you will face various temptations
and must meet these in the strength of the Lord. Among
these will be loneliness, stubborness, impatience with
married couples (especially if you are expected to be a
babysitter), the feeling that you will be pushed from one
station or area of service to another whenever a need for
a worker arises, the awful anticipation of being accommo-
dated with a family or married couple with little opportunity for privacy, and that strong, overpowering desire
for marriage and a home. All of these feelings come
occasionally to most single people. But compensations
come from the liberty you will have of entering fully
into His service, available at anytime to anyone without
reservation.

Single candidates should be stable people. You must
know how to bear responsibility. You must be able to use
authority, for if you are not in an administrative positic
during the course of your years with the mission, you will
surely have a maid, cook, or sweeper to whom you will need
to issue orders. You may have a way of being either too
dogmatic and authoritative, or lacking in these qualities
entirely. It is especially important for you to become
aware of others and their feelings.

Discretion should be used in your platform presentatic
Personal references should not be an advertisement. A
single girl who said publicly from the platform "I'm prayi

that God will give me a man before I go to the mission field" found a gentleman, twice her age and with one marriage already behind him, proposing to her after the service. When she refused, he followed her to several churches where she was scheduled to speak, and eventually travelled several hundred miles to her home to ask for her hand in marriage. She learned her lesson and thereafter made her request known only to God!

You must be careful to keep yourself from unsuitable friendships involving those who do not seek to give God glory in their lives. Strong attachments of this type have resulted in loss of effective Christian witness.

You must guard yourself against volunteering for more than you can effectively accomplish. You may even accept too heavy a deputation schedule, or assume too many responsibilities for the Mission. Normally you will not be able to carry as strenuous a load on the field as you can in the homeland. Learn your limitations.

Don't envy your married colleagues. Don't make fun of marriage. Don't expect to always be included in groups of couples. Don't be discouraged when you can't brag about your children. Throughout your deputation meetings, ever be sure you have an answer that fully satisfies your own heart when you are asked the question, "Why aren't you married?" If you can't give a good answer, think about it for a while. It will be asked a good many times at home, and will surely be asked on the field by nationals who often cannot understand such a status since it is in opposition to their whole way of life.

The mission field may provide a mate for you. But make absolutely certain that this is God's will for you. Don't spend time and energy seeking a wife when you should be searching for lost souls, or hunting a husband when you could be heralding His grace. "Seek ye first the kingdom of God and His righteousness; and all these things shall be added unto you"[1] - as much as you need for the work to which you are dedicating your life.

[1] Matthew 6:33

"No good thing will He withhold from them that walk uprightly."[1]

If you are single, thank God for it. If you are married, befriend the single folks. They need your loving concern. And may you be completely content in whatever state you find yourself. God can and will use you in His service.

[1] Psalm 84:11

22

Children Of
Accepted Candidates

Mission Boards have sometimes received letters of
inquiry stating, "My wife is opposed to my decision to
be a missionary, but I'm going ahead with it anyway."
One lady, with no qualms, appeared in a mission office
stating, "My husband didn't want to go so I left him
home with the children, but I am ready for you to send
me to the field immediately." We smile at those who
actually believe they are following the Lord by cutting
off a mate who doesn't have a "call" to the mission
field, or those who volunteer to serve in order to get
out of a situation which cannot be solved.

But what about the children in your family? Are
they considered in your decision?

"Oh", but you say "they are too young to know" or
"they can't make this decision for us." In many cases
this is, and ought to be true. No one on earth has
the authority to dictate the will of God to another,
and therefore a decision to become a missionary family
has rested entirely with you.

Before you applied to a mission, you should have
prayerfully considered the pros and cons of raising
a family on the field. If you are only now planning your
family, or if your children are very young, they would,
of course, abide by your decision. (Even so, you will
do well to consider the health factors that will be
involved, any disability your child may have, psychological
problems which may be developing and your own reaction
to bringing up these little ones in a land which may be

less sanitary than your own, with children of a different culture, language and thought patterns, and the long separations which may be involved if children are sent away to school).

But for children who are aware of the world around them, those who have already begun to choose their friends, their likes and dislikes, and more especially, those teen-agers who have found it difficult to adjust to the various physical and psychological changes in their growth without the further problem of adjusting to a completely new way of living, it is logical to follow the command of the Word which directs us to "do all things decently and in order" (I Corinthians 14:40).

Your call to the mission field, backed by the Word of God and the assurance of His Spirit must dominate the entire life of the family. Children ought to be sub-ject to the decisions of their parents. But a rebellious child at home could be obnoxious and troublesome on the field. If you cannot discipline your child in the home, it is not really fair to expect that a missionary teacher can make him docile and satisfied. (It has and can be done, but it should raise serious questions in your mind). If there is any tendency toward unnatural dependence and instability or other psychological disturbances, pro-fessional help should be obtained in determining the child's ability to cope with the drastic changes which will come to him as an M.K.

One of the main factors in the child's adjustment to life itself and the possibility of being raised on the mission field is the parents' attitude toward the call and service of God. Despondent, discouraged, unstable, complaining parents will find that their children will not readily adjust to change. Those who go about their work optimistically, zealously, lovingly, without the constant feeling of making a tremendous sacrifice will find their children enjoying this new open door of their lives.

Children should be helped to understand the importance and urgency of missionary work. They should have a share in the family life. They must never be left out to such an extent that they feel mother and dad always have time for supporting churches, nationals, other missionaries

and mission problems, but never time or concern for them.
(Your deputation ministry will help you to work out the
problem of spending time with the family).

Children are sometimes forced to speak or sing in
public during days of deputation. Some children thrive
on this, but others are embarrassed by it. Forcing the
children to participate can have severely adverse
effects on them. Other children will feel left out if
they do not have a part in the program. A son and
daughter of a missionary couple felt so much a part of
the total presentation that when the annual Mission I.D.
cards were sent to the parents, the teen-agers questioned
why they didn't receive cards, too. What a joy to a
family to see their children considering themselves not
as children of missionaries, but as actually a part of
the mission.

Your children should be taught discipline and they
should be disciplined, both because it is Biblical, and
because it can save you from a good many awkward and
unhappy situations with co-workers on the field in the
days ahead. And they will have many aunties and uncles
to contend with in the years to come!

In many instances, missionary children develop the
idea that they must always wear the worn out or grown out
clothing left over from more well-to-do children in the
homeland. (Unfortunately, this has sometimes been true).
There are times when there may be too much frugality on
the part of parents when it comes to clothing their
children and providing those few little extras that mean
so much to all children (and adults) everywhere.

These youngsters need to be allowed to live a normal,
happy life. They are no different than other children
their age and should not be made to feel that they must
abide by altogether different principles. Commit them
daily to the Lord. Instruct them and teach them in the
Word of God. Love them and don't be afraid to express
your love for them. Show by your own life that Christianity means something to you, and is, in fact, the most
important thing in your life. You may be able to fool the
nationals or your co-workers, but you will never deceive
your children. They know what you are before coffee in
the morning, after the ninth interruption during your

message preparation, when you come home exhausted trying to determine why the antenna switching system didn't work well, and they see and hear your reactions to mission plans and policies. Your life is the greatest influence in the lives of your children. Your reactions will mold their thinking.

Then, too, do you really feel you can trust your children to the Lord's keeping when an epidemic of typhoid sweeps through your area, when they are 500 miles away in Boarding School, or 10,000 miles away in college? Do you have the patience to teach your children if there is no opportunity to send them to school? Can you help them adjust to a new situation to which you, yourself, are not fully acclimated?

Perhaps your children are excited about the prospects of moving to a foreign land. It may sound like a thrillin adventure. But they must understand, if they are old enough, that this adventure is going to last a good many years. They should study about the country to which they are going. They should read good missionary books. You should encourage them and lead them in enthusiasm.

People often ask if there aren't too many disadvantages to consider taking children to the field. Some newlyweds even question the adviseability of having a family at all if they are to serve the Lord in a foreign country.

Actually, there are far more advantages than disadvantages to the well-adjusted M.K. The educational level of most schools for missionary children is very high; the culture, customs, history and language of the country is broadening; friendships with young people from other lands is stimulating; the knowledge that mother and dad are "serving the Lord" is spiritually invigorating; seeing the changed lives of those who believe is encouragi having a part in tract distribution and other vital witnes is rewarding; proving the promises of God from day to day is strengthening.

You will not be able to determine accurately your child's endurance level before you are actually in a missi field situation. But do not neglect the consideration of these young lives committed to you as you prepare for service. They are your first responsibility. And then, having found His will in the matter, go forth in His strength. There will be many trials and discouragements along the way, but what greater thrill could come to a missionary mother and dad than to see a son or daughter return to the mission field for service, or to serve the Lord as a dedicated Christian in the homeland? To a large extent, it all depends upon YOU.

23

Bon Voyage

The final step before leaving for service entails
the very difficult matter of fond farewells to friends
and relatives. In some instances, this will not be
accomplished without a very large quantity of the grace
of God. For others, parting, although never easy, is
the threshhold to greater joys than have ever before
been anticipated or experienced, and in the expectation
of all that lies ahead, the temporary parting is made
peacefully and swiftly.

Among the most difficult departures are those who
must leave a very ill family member, a loved one who
will not join you on the field for another year or two,
those who have depended heavily upon their circle of
friends and loved ones and do not find it easy to adjust
to new friends, and those who leave without the blessing
of their family upon them (many being callous and
indifferent to the Gospel and thoroughly opposed to the
step now being taken).

Send-offs can be quiet and quick, or they can result
in a large delegation of well-wishers saying endless
"God Bless You's". These moments will long be remembered
by all concerned and there is, in some,that last quiet
question of what one has left and what may lie ahead.
Then the kisses done with, and the hand waving no longer
visible, the missionary candidate speeds forth to that
wide open door which God has chosen for him to enter.

May His highest and best blessings be yours as you ente
with Him and with your fellow-laborers, His field of servic
for you.

24

Bibliography

The books listed herewith in their various categories
are not, by any means, the only ones available for your
reading. Your Board will be able to advise you concerning
books which they feel will be especially beneficial to
you in preparation for your particular field. But this
selected list will give you an overall view of the various
facets of missionary life which will help you to obtain
a fuller understanding of your part in the Great Commission.

HISTORY OF MISSIONS

Cook, Harold R. Highlights of Christian Missions. Chicago:
Moody Press, 1967.

Edman, V. Raymond. The Light in Dark Ages. Wheaton:
VanKampen Press, 1949.

Kane, J. Herbert. A Global View of Christian Missions
from Pentecost to the Present. Grand Rapids: Baker
Book House, 1971. (The Bibliography included in this
book is excellent).

Glover, Robert Hall. The Progress of World-Wide Missions.
Revised and enlarged by J. Herbert Kane. New York:
Harper, 1960

Latourette, Kenneth Scott. Christianity Through the Ages.
New York: Harper & Row, 1965.

MISSIONARY PREPARATION

Beyerhaus, Peter and Lefever, Henry. The Responsible
    Church and the Foreign Mission. Grand Rapids:
    Eerdman, 1964.

Brown, Arthur Judson. The Foreign Missionary. New York:
    Fleming H. Revell Company, 1907.

Cable, Mildred and French, Francesca. Ambassadors for
    Christ. Hodder and Stoughton, 1937.

Cook, Harold R. Missionary Life and Work. Chicago:
    Moody Press, 1959.

Cook, Harold R. An Introduction to the Study of Christian
    Missions. Chicago: Moody Press, 1954.

Ford, Leighton. The Christian Persuader. New York:
    Harper & Row, 1966.

Glover, Robert Hall. The Bible Basis of Missions. Los
    Angeles, 1946.

Hill, Frances M. Missionary Education of Children.
    Philadelphia: Judson Press, 1963.

Hogben, Rowland. In Training. Inter-Varsity Christian
    Fellowship, 1946.

Houghton, A. Preparing to be a Missionary. Chicago:
    Inter-Varsity Press, 1956.

Mostert, John. The Preparation of a Missionary. Wheaton,
    Ill.: Accrediting Association of Bible Colleges, 1968.

Nida, Eugene A. Religion Across Cultures. New York:
    Harper & Row, 1968.

Nida, Eugene A. and Smalley, William A. Introducing
    Animism. New York: Friendship Press, 1959.

Seamands, John T. The Supreme Task of the Church. Grand
    Rapids: Eerdmans, 1964.

Smith, Oswald J. The Passion for Souls. London:
  Marshall, Morgan and Scott, 1950.

Soltau, T. Stanley. Facing the Field. Grand Rapids:
  Baker Book House, 1959.

Strachan, R. Kenneth. The Inescapable Calling. Grand
  Rapids: Eerdmans, 1968.

Sundkler, Bengt. The World of Mission. Grand Rapids:
  Eerdmans, 1965.

Tuggy, Joy T. The Missionary Wife and Her Work. Chicago:
  Moody Press, 1966.

Zwemer, Samuel M. "Into All The World". Zondervan, 1943.

MISSIONARY PRINCIPLES AND PRACTICES

Allen, Roland. Missionary Principles. Grand Rapids:
  Eerdmans, 1964.

Lindsell, Harold. Missionary Principles and Practice.
  Westwood, N.J.: Fleming H. Revell, 1955.

Ritchie, John. Indigenous Church Principles in Theory and
  Practice. New York: Fleming H. Revell Company, 1946.

Zwemer, Samuel M. Thinking Missions with Christ. Grand
  Rapids: Zondervan, 1934.

CHANGING MISSIONARY METHODS

Bridston, Keth R. Shock and Renewal: The Christian
  Mission Enters a New Era. Published for the Student
  Volunteer Movement for Christian Missions by
  Friendship Press, 1955.

Cook, Harold R. Strategy of Missions: An Evangelical
  View. Chicago: Moody Press, 1963.

Fife, Eric S. and Glasser, Arthur F. Missions in Crisis;
    Rethinking Missionary Strategy. Chicago: Inter-
    Varsity Press, 1961.

Higdon, E. K. New Missionaries for New Days. St. Louis:
    The Bethany Press, 1956.

Howard, David M. Student Power in World Evangelism.
    Downers Grove, Ill.: Inter-Varsity, 1970.

McGavran, Donald A., ed., Church Growth and Christian
    Mission. New York: Harper & Row, 1965.

Rees, Paul S. Don't Sleep Through the Revolution. Waco,
    Texas: Word Books, 1970.

Soltau, T. Stanley. Missions at the Crossroads. Wheaton:
    VanKampen, 1954.

MISSIONARY PROBLEMS

Adolph, Paul E. Missionary Health Manual. Chicago:
    Moody Press, 1959.

Bailey, Helen L. A Study of Missionary Motivation, Train-
    ing and Withdrawal (1953-1962). New York: Missionary
    Research Library, 1965.

Fey, Harold E., ed. A History of the Ecumenical Movement:
    1948-1968. Philadelphia: Westminster Press, 1970.

Isais, Juan M. The Other Side of the Coin. Grand Rapids:
    Eerdmans, 1966.

Neill, Stephen. Colonialism and Christian Missions.
    London: Lutterworth Press, 1966.

Scherer, James A. Missionary, Go Home! Englewood Cliffs,
    N.J.: Prentice Hall, 1964.

Soltau, T. Stanley. Facing the Field; The Foreign
    Missionary and His Problems. Grand Rapids: Baker
    Book House, 1959.

Williamson, Mabel. "Have We No Right...?" Chicago: Moody Press, 1957.

MISSIONARY BIOGRAPHIES

Again it should be mentioned that this is only a partial listing of books which could be included here. Be sure to search out biographies concerning your special field of service.

Bach, Thomas J. Pioneer Missionaries for Christ and His Church. Wheaton, Ill.: VanKampen Press, 1955.

Edwards, Jonathan, ed. The Life and Diary of David Brainerd. Chicago: Moody Press, 1949.

Elliot, Elisabeth. Shadow of the Almighty: The Life and Testament of Jim Elliot. New York: Harper & Row, 1958.

Elliot, Elisabeth. Who Shall Ascend? (R. Kenneth Strachan, Costa Rica). New York: Harper & Row, 1968.

Goforth, Rosalind. Goforth of China. Zondervan, 1937.

Kellersberger, Julia Lake and Eugene. Doctor of the Happy Landings. Richmond, Va.: John Knox Press, 1949.

Judson, Edward. The Life of Adoniram Judson. Philadelphia: American Baptist Publication, 1883.

Mueller, J. Theodore. John G. Paton; Missionary to the New Hebrides. Zondervan, 1941.

Paton, William. Alexander Duff, Pioneer of Missionary Education. New York: George H. Doran Co., 1923.

Pearson, B. H. The Monk Who Lived Again. Light and Life Press, 1944.

Petersen, William J. Another Hand on Mine. New York: McGraw Hill, 1967. (Dr. Carl Becker, A.I.M.).

Taylor, Mrs. Howard. Behind the Ranges: Fraser of
   Lisuland. London: Lutterworth Press (n.d.)

Taylor, Mrs. Howard. The Triumph of John and Betty
   Stam. China Inland Mission, 1935.

Taylor, Dr. and Mrs. Howard. Hudson Taylor in Early
   Years; the growth of a soul. China Inland Mission:
   1911.

Wilson, J. Christy. Apostle to Islam; A biography of
   Samuel M. Zwemer. Grand Rapids: Baker Book
   House, 1952.

SPECIALIZED MISSIONS

Cook, Frank S. Seeds in the Wind. Quito, Ecuador:
   The World Radio Missionary Fellowship, Inc., 1961.

Kane, J. Herbert. Faith Mighty Faith. Missionary
   Aviation Fellowship, 1956.

Nida, Eugene A. Message and Mission. New York:
   Harper, 1960.

Wallis, Ethel E. Two Thousand Tongues to Go. New York:
   Harper, 1959.

SPECIFIC MISSION FIELD AREAS

Andersson, Efraim. Churches at the Grass Roots: A
   Study in Congo-Brazzaville. London: Lutterworth,
   1968.

Anderson, Gerald H., ed. Studies in Philippine Church
   History. Ithaca, N.Y.: Cornell University Press,
   1969.

Bulifant, Josephine C. Forty Years in the African Bush.
   Grand Rapids: Zondervan, 1950.

Carmichael, Amy. Mimosa. London: Society for Promoting
    Christian Knowledge, 1949.

Crawford, David and Leona. Missionary Adventures in
    the South Pacific. Rutland, Vt.: Tuttle, 1967.

Davis, Raymond J. Fire on the Mountains (the study of
    a miracle - the Church in Ethiopia). Grand Rapids:
    Zondervan, 1966.

Dowdy, Homer E. The Bamboo Cross. (Christian witness
    in the jungles of Vietnam). New York: Harper & Row,
    1965.

Drown, Frank and Marie. Mission to the Headhunters.
    (Ecuador). New York: Harper & Row, 1961.

Drummond, Richard H. A History of Christianity in Japan.
    Grand Rapids: Eerdmans, 1970.

Eby, Omar. Whisper in a Dry Land. (Somalia). Winona
    Lake, Ind.: Herald, 1968.

Elliot, Elisabeth. The Savage My Kinsman. New York:
    Harper & Brothers, 1961.

Evans, Robert B. Let Europe Hear. Chicago: Moody
    Press, 1964.

Fish, Eric G. The Prickly Pear. London: Marshall,
    Morgan and Scott, 1951.

Fuller, Harold W. Aftermath: The Dramatic Rebirth
    of Eastern Nigeria. New York: Sudan Interior
    Mission, 1970.

Glover, Archibald E. A Thousand Miles of Miracle in
    China. London: Pickering and Inglis, Ltd., 1945.

Gonzales, Justo L. The Development of Christianity in
    the Latin Caribbean. Grand Rapids: Eerdmans, 1969.

Groves, C. P. The Planting of Christianity in Africa
    1840-1954. 4 volumes. London: Lutterworth,
    1948-1958.

Gunther, Peter F., Ed. The Fields at Home: Studies in Home Missions. Chicago: Moody Press, 1963.

Hitt, Russel T. Cannibal Valley. (West Irian). New York: Harper & Row, 1962.

Howard, David M. Hammered as Gold. (Colombia). New York: Harper & Row, 1969.

Johnson, Harmon A. The Growing Church in Haiti. Coral Gables, Fla.: West Indies Mission, 1970.

Kuhn, Isobel. Nests Above the Abyss. Philadelphia: China Inland Mission, 1947.

Kuhn, Isobel. Stones of Fire. Philadelphia: China Inland Mission, 1951.

Lageer, Eileen. New Life for All. (Nigeria). Chicago: Moody, 1970.

Lee, Robert. Stranger in the Land: A Study of the Church in Japan. London: Lutterworth, 1967.

Lyall, Leslie T. Come Wind, Come Weather. Chicago: Moody Press, 1960.

Lyall, Leslie T. Mission Fields Today: A Brief World Survey. London: Inter-Varsity Fellowship, 1963.

Lyall, Leslie T. Red Sky at Night. Waco, Texas: Word Books, 1969.

Lyall, Leslie T. Urgent Harvest. London: China Inland Mission, 1961.

McGavran, Donald. Church Growth in Mexico. Grand Rapids: Eerdmans, 1963.

Mbiti, John S. African Religions and Philosophy. London: Heinemann, 1969.

Neill, Stephen. The Story of the Christian Church in India and Pakistan. Grand Rapids: Eerdmans, 1970.

Nickel, Ben J. Along the Quichua Trail. Smithville,
    Mo.: Gospel Missionary Union, 1965.

Patterson, George N. Christianity in Communist China.
    Waco, Texas: Word Books, 1969.

Porterfield, Bruce E. Commandos for Christ. (Bolivia).
    New York: Harper & Row, 1963.

Richter, Julius. A History of Protestant Missions in
    the Near East. New York: Revell, 1910.

Read, William R., Monterroso, Victor M., and Johnson,
    Harmon A. Church Growth in Latin America. Grand
    Rapids: Eerdmans, 1969.

Read, William R., New Patterns of Church Growth in
    Brazil. Grand Rapids: Eerdmans, 1965.

Sales, Jane M. The Planting of Churches in South Africa.
    Grand Rapids: Eerdmans, 1971.

Smith, Mrs. Gordon H. Victory in Viet Nam. Grand Rapids:
    Zondervan, 1965.

Shearer, Roy E. Wildfire Church Growth in Korea. Grand
    Rapids: Eerdmans, 1966.

Spain, Mildred W. "And In Samaria". Dallas: The Central
    America Mission, printed by Banks, Upshaw and Co.,
    Dallas, 1954.

Sundkler, Bengt. The Christian Ministry in Africa.
    London: SCM Press, 1962.

Wall, Martha. Splinters from an African Log. Chicago:
    Moody Press, 1960.

Wallis, Ethel E. The Dayuma Story. New York: Harper & Row,
    1960.

Warren, T.J.P. North Africa Today. Tunis: North Africa
    Mission, 1947.

Wold, Joseph C. God's Impatience in Liberia. Grand
    Rapids: Eerdmans, 1967.

Evangelical Foreign Missions Association. *Annual Report*. 1405 G. St., N.W., Washington, D.C. 20005

Interdenominational Foreign Mission Association. *Annual Report*. 54 Bergen Ave., Ridgefield Park, N.J. 07660.

MISSIONARY IMPACT

Bavinck, Dr. J. H. The Impact of Christianity on the Non-Christian World. Grand Rapids: Eerdmans, 1948.

Kraemer, Hendrik. The Christian Message in a Non-Christian World. New York: Harper and Brothers, 1947.

Lindsell, Harold, ed. Congress on the Church's Worldwide Mission, Wheaton, Ill. 1966. Waco, Texas: Word Books, 1966.

MISSIONARY AGENCIES

Goddard, Burton L., ed. The Encyclopedia of Modern Christian Missions: The Agencies. Camden, N.J.: Nelson, 1967.

Kane, J. Herbert. A Global View of Christian Missions from Pentecost to the Present. Grand Rapids: Baker Book House, 1971.

MISSIONARY BOOKS FOR YOUNG PEOPLE

Miller, Basil. Nineteen Missionary Stories from the Middle East. Grand Rapids: Zondervan, 1950.

Miller, Basil. Twenty Missionary Stories from Africa. Grand Rapids: Zondervan, 1951.

Miller, Basil. Twenty Missionary Stories from India. Grand Rapids: Zondervan, 1952.

Miller, Basil. Twenty Missionary Stories from Latin
    America. Grand Rapids: Zondervan, 1951.

Miller, Basil. Ann Judson: Heroine of Burma. Grand
    Rapids: Zondervan, 1947.

Miller, Basil. Wilfred Grenfell; Labrador's Dogsled
    Doctor. Grand Rapids: Zondervan, 1948.

For those going to Africa, the Jungle Doctor Series
authored by Dr. Paul White and published by Moody Press
are highly recommended.

BIBLE REFERENCE BOOKS

It is suggested that the following reference books
be taken with you to the field, or others of equal
content and calibre.

Halley, Henry H. Halley's Bible Handbook. Grand Rapids:
    Zondervan, 1962.

Jamieson, Rev. Robert, Fausset, Rev. A. R., Brown, Rev.
    David. Commentary on the Whole Bible. Grand
    Rapids: Zondervan, (n.d.)

Stevens, Wm. Arnold and Burton, Ernest DeWitt. A Harmony
    of the Gospels. New York: Charles Scribner's Sons,
    1932.

Strong, Augustus Hopkins. Systematic Theology. Phila-
    delphia: The Judson Press, 1907.

Thompson, Frank Charles, comp. & ed. The New Chain
    Reference Bible. Indianapolis: B. B. Kirkbride
    Bible Co., 1934.

Unger, Merrill F. Unger's Bible Dictionary. Chicago:
    Moody Press, 1965.

Unger, Merrill F. Unger's Bible Handbook. Chicago:
    Moody Press, 1966.

Vollmer, Philip. The Modern Student's Life of Christ.
New York: Fleming H. Revell Co., 1912.

Along with these reference books, be sure to take a
good Dictionary, and an encyclopedia, if one is available
to you. (This is especially essential if you plan to
teach your own children on the field).

DEVOTIONAL BOOKS

Perhaps you have devotional books which you have
used in the homeland for several years. Be sure to
take those to the field with you. Be careful to take a
variety. Among those which you may choose are:

My Utmost for His Highest by Oswald Chambers

Daily Light

Morning and Evening by C. H. Spurgeon

Streams in the Desert by Mrs. Charles E. Cowman

Springs in the Valley by Mrs. Charles E. Cowman

Any of Amy Carmichael's many volumes

You should also plan to take several versions of
the Scriptures for both study and devotions.

GENERAL REFERENCE BOOKS

Those who will be serving in specialized fields in
a professional capacity will take reference books pertinent to your sphere of service. Perhaps this will
include music books, a Secretary's Handbook, books on
engineering, bookkeeping, administration, photography,
radio, medicine, television, education, children's work
(including a good Bible story book), building, mechanics,
or cookbooks with simple recipes using basic foods.

Every doctor and nurse should have the latest copy

of the Physician's Desk Reference (PDR).

Each household should have a good First Aid book.

For those who will be involved in Christian Education, The Modern Practice of Adult Education (by Malcolm S. Knowles. New York: Association Press, 1970), will prove to be invaluable.

A last minute browse through your local Christian Bookstore may prove profitable to you. Seek out books which may be of particular help to you or your children as you set your face toward the field.

NOTES